Practice*Planners*

Arthur E. Jongsma, Jr., Series Editor

Helping therapists help their clients...

Treatment Planners cover all the necessary elements for developing formal treatment plans, including detailed problem definitions, long-term goals, short-term objectives, therapeutic interventions, and DSM-IV™ diagnoses.

D1219247

The **Complete Trea**..eries of books combines our bestselling *Treatmen*................................o one easy-to-use, all-in-one resource for mental h................................ring from the most commonly diagnosed disorders.

Over 500,000 Practice*Planners* sold . . .

WILEY

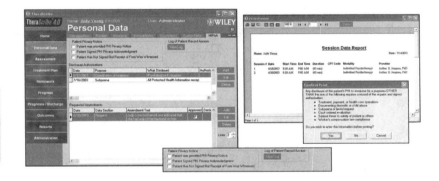

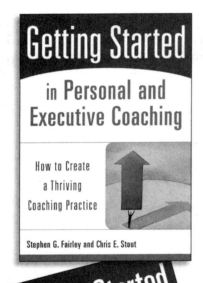

The Early Childhood Education Intervention Treatment Planner

Practice*Planners*® Series

Treatment Planners

The Complete Adult Psychotherapy Treatment Planner, Third Edition
The Child Psychotherapy Treatment Planner, Third Edition
The Adolescent Psychotherapy Treatment Planner, Third Edition
The Addiction Treatment Planner, Third Edition
The Continuum of Care Treatment Planner
The Couples Psychotherapy Treatment Planner
The Employee Assistance Treatment Planner
The Pastoral Counseling Treatment Planner
The Older Adult Psychotherapy Treatment Planner
The Behavioral Medicine Treatment Planner
The Group Therapy Treatment Planner, Second Edition
The Gay and Lesbian Psychotherapy Treatment Planner
The Family Therapy Treatment Planner
The Severe and Persistent Mental Illness Treatment Planner
The Mental Retardation and Developmental Disability Treatment Planner
The Social Work and Human Services Treatment Planner
The Crisis Counseling and Traumatic Events Treatment Planner
The Personality Disorders Treatment Planner
The Rehabilitation Psychology Treatment Planner
The Special Education Treatment Planner
The Juvenile Justice and Residential Care Treatment Planner
The School Counseling and School Social Work Treatment Planner
The Sexual Abuse Victim and Sexual Offender Treatment Planner
The Probation and Parole Treatment Planner
The Psychopharmacology Treatment Planner
The Speech-Language Pathology Treatment Planner
The Suicide and Homicide Risk Assessment & Prevention Treatment Planner
The College Student Counseling Treatment Planner
The Parenting Skills Treatment Planner
The Early Childhood Education Intervention Treatment Planner
The Co-occurring Disorders Treatment Planner

Progress Notes Planners

The Child Psychotherapy Progress Notes Planner, Second Edition
The Adolescent Psychotherapy Progress Notes Planner, Second Edition
The Adult Psychotherapy Progress Notes Planner, Second Edition
The Addiction Progress Notes Planner
The Severe and Persistent Mental Illness Progress Notes Planner
The Couples Psychotherapy Progress Notes Planner
The Family Therapy Progress Notes Planner

Homework Planners

Brief Therapy Homework Planner
Brief Couples Therapy Homework Planner
Brief Adolescent Therapy Homework Planner
Brief Child Therapy Homework Planner
Brief Employee Assistance Homework Planner
Brief Family Therapy Homework Planner
Grief Counseling Homework Planner
Group Therapy Homework Planner
Divorce Counseling Homework Planner
School Counseling and School Social Work Homework Planner
Child Therapy Activity and Homework Planner
Addiction Treatment Homework Planner, Second Edition
Adolescent Psychotherapy Homework Planner II
Adult Psychotherapy Homework Planner
Parenting Skills Homework Planner

Client Education Handout Planners

Adult Client Education Handout Planner
Child and Adolescent Client Education Handout Planner
Couples and Family Client Education Handout Planner

Complete Planners

The Complete Depression Treatment and Homework Planner
The Complete Anxiety Treatment and Homework Planner

PracticePlanners®

Arthur E. Jongsma, Jr., Series Editor

The Early Childhood Education Intervention Treatment Planner

Julie A. Winkelstern

Arthur E. Jongsma, Jr.

WILEY

JOHN WILEY & SONS, INC.

Copyright © 2006 by Julie A. Winkelstern and Arthur E. Jongsma, Jr. All rights reserved.

Published by John Wiley & Sons, Inc., Hoboken, New Jersey.
Published simultaneously in Canada.

For general information on our other products and services please contact our Customer Care Department within the United States at (800) 762-2974, outside the United States at (317) 572-3993 or fax (317) 572-4002.

Wiley also publishes its books in a variety of electronic formats. Some content that appears in print may not be available in electronic books. For more information about Wiley products, visit our web site at www.wiley.com.

All references to diagnostic codes are reprinted with permission from the *Diagnostic and Statistical Manual of Mental Disorders, Fourth Edition, Text Revision.* Copyright © 2000 American Psychiatric Association.

Library of Congress Cataloging-in-Publication Data
Winkelstern, Julie A.
    The early childhood intervention treatment planner / Julie Winkelstern, Arthur E. Jongsma, Jr.
        p. cm. — (Practiceplanners series)
    Includes bibliographical references.
    ISBN-13: 978-0-471-65962-4 (pbk. : alk. paper)
    ISBN-10: 0-471-65962-2 (pbk. : alk. paper)
    1. Child psychotherapy. 2. Adolescent psychotherapy. I. Jongsma, Arthur E., 1943–. II. Title. III. Series: Practiceplanners.
    [DNLM: 1. Developmental Disabilities—diagnosis—Child—Handbooks. 2. Developmental Disabilities—diagnosis—Infant—Handbooks. 3. Developmental Disabilities—prevention & control—Child—Handbooks. 4. Developmental Disabilities—prevention & control—Infant—Handbooks. 5. Early Intervention (Education)—Child—Handbooks. 6. Early Intervention (Education)—Infant—Handbooks. 7. Patient Care Planning—methods—Child. 8. Patient Care Planning—methods—Infant. WS 350.6 W774e 2006]
    RJ504.W56 2006
    618.92′8914—dc22
                                        2005019913

Printed in the United States of America.

10 9 8 7 6 5 4 3 2 1

To my long-standing friends Sandy Allers, Diane Harte, Loretta Metcalf, Kathleen Spencer, and Carol Wyskowski, who have been very fine advocates for children in their own right. To Lisa Leonard, childcare director extraordinaire, who has long known the gifts of providing quality care for young children. To the memory of Elma Wilson, who was an outstanding support to young children and their families, and who gave me ideas and inspiration for this book. And to the memory of Charlene Russell, who clearly understood the joys of working with young children with disabilities.

—J. A. W.

To my daughter, Kendra van Elst, a professional early childhood educator who senses what is best for children far beyond what she was ever taught—she is a natural.

—A. E. J.

CONTENTS

PRACTICE*PLANNERS*® SERIES PREFACE

The practice of psychotherapy has a dimension that did not exist 30, 20, or even 15 years ago—accountability. Treatment programs, public agencies, clinics, and even group and solo practitioners must now justify the treatment of patients to outside review entities that control the payment of fees. This development has resulted in an explosion of paperwork. Clinicians must now document what has been done in treatment, what is planned for the future, and what the anticipated outcomes of the interventions are. The books and software in this Practice*Planners* series are designed to help practitioners fulfill these documentation requirements efficiently and professionally.

The Practice*Planners* series has grown rapidly. It now includes not only the original *Complete Adult Psychotherapy Treatment Planner,* Third Edition, *The Child Psychotherapy Treatment Planner,* Third Edition, and *The Adolescent Psychotherapy Treatment Planner,* Third Edition, but also Treatment Planners targeted to specialty areas of practice, including: addictions, co-occurring disorders, juvenile justice/residential care, couples therapy, employee assistance, behavioral medicine, therapy with older adults, pastoral counseling, family therapy, group therapy, neuropsychology, therapy with gays and lesbians, special education, school counseling, probation and parole, therapy with sexual abuse victims and offenders, and more.

Several of the Treatment Planner books now have companion Progress Notes Planners (e.g., Adult, Adolescent, Child, Addictions, Severe and Persistent Mental Illness, Couples, Family). These planners provide a menu of progress statements that elaborate on the client's symptom presentation and the provider's therapeutic intervention. Each Progress Notes Planner statement is directly integrated with "Behavioral Definitions" and "Therapeutic Interventions" items from the companion Treatment Planner.

The list of therapeutic Homework Planners has grown to include Adult, Adolescent, Child, Couples, Group, Family, Addictions, Divorce, Grief, Employee Assistance, School Counseling/School Social Work Homework Planners, and Parenting Skills. Each of these books can be used alone or in conjunction with their companion Treatment Planner. Homework assignments are designed around each presenting problem (e.g., Anxiety, Depression, Chemical Dependence, Anger Management, Panic, Eating Disorders) that is the focus of a chapter in its corresponding Treatment Planner.

Client Education Handout Planners, a new branch in the series, provides brochures and handouts to help educate and inform adult, child, adolescent, couples, and family clients on a myriad of mental health issues, as well as life-skills techniques. The list of presenting problems for which information is provided mirrors the list of presenting problems in the Treatment Planner of the title similar to that of the Handout Planner. Thus, the problems for which educational material is provided in the *Child and Adolescent Client Education Handout Planner* reflect the presenting problems listed in *The Child* and *The Adolescent Psychotherapy Treatment Planner* books. Handouts are included on CD-ROMs for easy printing and are ideal for use in waiting rooms, at presentations, as newsletters, or as information for clients struggling with mental illness issues.

In addition, the series also includes Thera*Scribe*®, the latest version of the popular treatment planning, clinical record-keeping software. Thera*Scribe* allows the user to import the data from any of the Treatment Planner, Progress Notes Planner, or Homework Planner books into the software's expandable database. Then the point-and-click method can create a detailed, neatly organized, individualized, and customized treatment plan along with optional integrated progress notes and homework assignments.

Adjunctive books, such as *The Psychotherapy Documentation Primer,* and *Clinical, Forensic, Child, Couples and Family, Continuum of Care,* and *Chemical Dependence Documentation Sourcebook* contain forms and resources to aid the mental health practice management. The goal of the series is to provide practitioners with the resources they need in order to provide high-quality care in the era of accountability—or, to put it simply, we seek to help you spend more time on patients, and less time on paperwork.

ARTHUR E. JONGSMA, JR.
Grand Rapids, Michigan

ACKNOWLEDGMENTS

It has been an exciting adventure being given the privilege to once again co-author a treatment planner with Dr. Art Jongsma as part of his distinguished Practice*Planner* series. He has been most supportive in recognizing the importance of this endeavor, understanding that every young child should have daily experiences, whether in the home, in a preschool, in a special education classroom, or in a daycare center that is based on developmentally appropriate best practices. There continues to be a great need to provide best-practice information to those professionals who have been given the considerable responsibility of instructing, guiding, comforting, and nurturing our young children. As a special education administrator, school psychologist, and former elementary teacher and childcare provider, I have been privileged to spend time with many talented professionals and many caring parents who have served as outstanding advocates for quality programming and care for all young children. My former related service staff and special education staff in the Forest Hills School District in Grand Rapids, Michigan were always inspiring to me, as they continually sought to bring excellence to their service to children. Lauren Radde, Kathy Anderson, and Diane Coleman taught me what it meant to be quality early childhood educators. My current related service staff at Eaton Intermediate School District in Charlotte, Michigan is exceptional, including Peg Cameron and the talented Early On professionals, who have shown me what true devotion to young children and families really means. My direct supervisor, Dr. Wayne Buletza, is very much dedicated to improving the lives of young children through his visionary scope and motivation. His daily encouragement and inspiration is greatly appreciated. I am thankful for and applaud the support I receive each workday from the administrative assistants in my office. Thank you to Erika duBois, Connie Mitchell, Robin Petersen, and Candice Abood.

I want to express my special and very sincere thanks to Art Jongsma for his considerable patience, ongoing support, creativity, encouragement, and vision in seeing this project to its completion. My particular thanks to Jennifer Byrne and Sue Rhoda for providing great attention to detail and outstanding organization to this manuscript. I gratefully thank all the talented staff at John

Wiley & Sons, especially David Bernstein and Judi Knott, for all their valuable support in making this book a reality. I additionally would like to recognize the support from my very fine brothers Robert and John, my wonderful sister-in-law, Carol, and my high-caliber nephews Brett and Dennis. Finally, I would like my very talented son, Ian, to know how very much I love him and am forever grateful for his continuing patience and sacrifice in living with his ever-driven mother.

—J. A. W.

My thanks to Julie Winkelstern for her expert contribution to the treatment planning literature. She understands young children and has wide experience in applying effective interventions in the education setting. Our Practice*Planner* series has been enriched by this book.

I am also grateful to my friend Dr. Garrett Boersma, who introduced me to the world of special education for very young children. His talents have led him from the special education classroom, to the college classroom, to the highest levels of special education administration—cream always rises to the top.

—A. E. J.

The Early Childhood Education Intervention Treatment Planner

INTRODUCTION

PLANNER FOCUS

The Early Childhood Education Intervention Treatment Planner is designed for all professionals and paraprofessionals working in various types of settings providing for the education and care of young children. These settings (among many) could include preschools, Head Start programs, early childhood centers, early childhood special education classrooms, daycare centers, and in-home childcare. This *Planner* can also be a tool for private clinicians working with families. The content of this text incorporates a multitude of presenting issues, some common and relatively minor but others very serious in nature, potentially altering or significantly interfering with the normal growth and development of the young child. The presenting problems are challenges faced by professionals and parents with an emphasis on how the organization and the family can effectively communicate and collaborate in the best interests of the child. The most common challenges for the young child, for the parents, and for professionals working with young children are targeted within each chapter. These include issues presenting in the physical, cognitive, affective, behavioral, social, and neurological domains.

Interventions have been designed to offer the early childhood specialist a variety of workable, constructive, realistic, and meaningful strategies to improve the quality of the child's classroom or daycare or home experience in a collaborative model involving the child, parents, and professionals. Emphasis is always placed on furthering the developmental progress of the young child as well as extending his or her independence and personal competency, regardless of the type or intensity of the condition or situation. While many interventions focus on the child's functioning in the classroom or daycare setting, others emphasize experiences in the home or across community settings, whether it be for social skill development, self-care, behavioral self-management, language accomplishments, pre-readiness, or fine and gross motor skills. Parents are encouraged to seek resources with support from the caring professionals involved with their child.

The writing of quality treatment plans for young children with specific conditions or disabilities based on specific, targeted areas of need can offer the early childhood specialist an essential tool in identifying meaningful and effective interventions. Further, it is our belief that in creating and following an individualized treatment plan, this process can enhance, and in many situations provide for optimum functioning, performance, and progress of the child.

HISTORY AND BACKGROUND

The inception and passage of the Education for All Handicapped Children Act (PL-142) in 1975 began a new era for students with disabilities in public schools in the United States. This federal law mandated the states to provide a free, appropriate public education for all children with disabilities beginning at age five, transforming the educational access and experiences of those with special needs. An amendment to the Education for All Handicapped Children Act in 1986 (PL-99-457) extended special education to all eligible children ages 3 to 5 years. This was landmark legislation for young children with disabilities and their families. Congress went on to change the name of the law to the Individuals with Disabilities Education Act (IDEA) in 1990 with another amendment (PL101-476). Reauthorization of the IDEA took place in 1997, outlining again for the states the requirements to provide a free, appropriate public education for all children with disabilities, ages 3 to 21 years of age. One of the major provisions identified in IDEA 97 mandates that children with disabilities are to be educated with their typically developing peers "to the maximum extent appropriate." Another major provision required that the evaluation process, when determining if the child is a child with a disability, include "a variety of assessment tools and strategies" when gathering functional and developmental data, and must include information provided by the parent. IDEA 97 specified that each child with a disability have an Individualized Educational Plan (IEP), which identified his or her goals and objectives and outlined programs and/or services (interventions) to meet the unique educational and learning needs of the child. Through the entire evaluation and IEP team process, emphasis must be placed on parental involvement. Specifically, the mandate of IDEA 97 strongly advocated that parents be involved in all decisions regarding their child's eligibility, placement, and services. Most recently, in November of 2004, the Individual Disabilities Education Improvement Act (IDEIA) was passed by Congress. The content of this legislation continues to emphasize full parental participation, as well as accountability and quality. Along with special education mandates, requirements governing other federal initiatives, such as the long-standing Head Start program, accentuate the importance of parental involvement.

This book focuses on parent participation in all chapters. Meaningful parental involvement is a potential element in all the treatment plans for all the disabilities and conditions in this text—throughout the consultation process, the evaluation process, the IEP team process, the implementation of programs, services, and interventions, and the general day-to-day communication between home and classroom/daycare setting. In effectively instructing or caring for any young child, establishing and maintaining a positive relationship of trust with both the child and the parents is imperative.

An increasing number of young children are in preschool and daycare settings in the United States, due to the greater number of two parents and single parents working outside the home. Thus, the need for research-based interventions to be used across early childhood settings would seem to be of even greater importance. Throughout this text, numerous, varied, and research-based interventions are identified that can offer the early childhood specialist developing a treatment plan unique developmental, physical, social, emotional, and cognitive attributes of the young child.

The therapeutic interventions in this text should be viewed as suggestions for consideration by the reader and are subject to required professional judgment, as each child, and each setting, warrants in-person, individualized consideration and attention.

All chapters begin and end with consultation with parents or primary caregivers as to the concerns regarding the child's functioning, and to promote an exchange of information between classroom/daycare and home. Evaluation is another important element of most chapters, which may involve specialists from the local public school agency, or from private clinicians or clinics, to include professionals such as counselors, special education early childhood teachers, school psychologists, clinical psychologists, child psychiatrists, behavioral specialists, school social workers, community mental health specialists, speech and language pathologists, occupational therapists, physical therapists, and/or teacher consultants. The goal of evaluation is to identify strengths and deficit areas of the young child, and then to coordinate treatment interventions to improve the child's functioning in the classroom/daycare setting, as well as in the home. Our purpose in writing this book is to support the educational specialist, the childcare provider, the private clinician, and parents and/or primary caregivers in clarifying and simplifying plans of intervention based on child needs.

TREATMENT PLAN UTILITY

Detailed, written early childhood treatment plans can benefit the child, the educational specialist, the childcare provider, the support team of related service providers, paraprofessionals, parents, as well as the educational and/or childcare setting and the greater community. The child is served by a written plan, as it stipulates the issues that are the focus of the treatment process. The focus of how to best serve the child in meeting his or her goals from an IEP, or how to developmentally move the child ahead in a preschool setting, and/or how to best care for a child with special needs or special conditions in a childcare setting or in the home, can be lost in the day-to-day logistics of a hectic, frequently interrupted, highly scheduled day. The treatment plan is a guide that structures the focus of the instructional and therapeutic interventions that are essential for the child to progress, to be safe, and to have his/her needs met. Since issues can change as the child's circumstances or needs change, the early childhood treatment plan must be viewed as a dynamic document that can, and must, be updated to reflect any major change of problem, definition, goal, objective, or intervention.

The child, parents, and the educators or providers for that child benefit from the early childhood treatment plan, which forces all to think carefully and directly about the desired outcomes. Behaviorally stated, measurable objectives clearly focus the instructional and/or childcare endeavor. The parents no longer have to wonder what is trying to be accomplished in the educational or childcare setting. Clear objectives allow those working with the child to channel their efforts into specific changes that will lead to long-term goals of problem resolution and/or improved functioning. Instructional and/or therapy support staff are concentrating on specifically stated objectives using specific interventions.

Staff is aided by early childhood treatment plans, as they are forced to think analytically and critically about the instructional and therapeutic interventions that are best suited for objective attainment for the child. The providers to the child must give advance attention to the technique or approach that will form the basis for an intervention.

A well-crafted treatment plan that clearly stipulates presenting problems, deficits, and intervention strategies facilitates the early childhood treatment process carried out by school team members in the special education classroom, instructional team members in the preschool setting, and childcare specialists in the daycare setting. Effective, well-defined communication among staff about what approaches are being implemented and who is responsible for which intervention is important. A thorough early childhood treatment plan stipulates *in writing* the details of the established objectives and the varied interventions, and can identify who will implement them.

Use of the early childhood treatment plan process as described in this text takes the early childhood special educator a step further past the writing of goals and objectives for the IEP. It provides a specific outline of support for the preschool or daycare staff, parents, or private clinician in working with the child. It can assist an early childhood professional in identifying the chosen interventions to be used and then communicating to others the specific method, means, format, sequential process, and/or creative experience by which the child will be assisted in eventually attaining positive outcomes.

HOW TO DEVELOP A TREATMENT PLAN

The process of developing a treatment plan involves a logical series of steps that build on each other, much like constructing a house. The foundation of any effective treatment plan is the data gathered within the course of the evaluation process. As part of the process prior to developing the treatment plan, the early childhood specialists must sensitively listen to and understand the struggles for the child in terms of learning deficits, emotional status, current stressors, social network, physical health, physical challenges, coping skills, self-esteem, family issues, and so on. It is imperative that assessment data be drawn from a variety of sources, which could include developmental and social history, physical exam, psychological testing, behavioral analysis, psychiatric evaluation/consultation, and evaluation in the therapy areas of occupational, physical, and language, with considerable attention to parent input throughout the evaluation process. The integration of the data is critical for understanding the child and his/her needs. We have identified five specific steps for developing an effective treatment plan.

Step One: Problem Selection

The professionals conducting an evaluation must ferret out the most significant problems on which to focus the early childhood treatment plan. Usually a primary problem will surface, and secondary problems certainly can be evident. Some other problems may have to be set aside as not urgent enough to require treatment at this time. An effective treatment plan can only deal with a few selected problems, or treatment will lose its direction. A variety of problems and conditions are represented as chapter titles within *The Early Childhood Education Intervention Treatment Planner.* Professional staff along with parents or primary caregivers may select those that most accurately represent the child's current and most salient needs.

As the problems to be selected become clear to the early childhood professionals and parents, it is important to consider input and responses from the child (as appropriate, dependent upon the child's age, mental status, and communication skills) as to the prioritization of issues or struggles. The child's motivation to participate in and cooperate with the treatment process needs to be an ongoing primary consideration of the team, always focusing on how the child's strengths and interests can be integrated into a plan that concentrates on improving deficit areas.

Step Two: Problem Definition

Each child presents with unique nuances as to how a problem or learning concern behaviorally reveals itself in his/her life. Therefore, each problem that is selected for treatment focus requires a specific definition about how it is evidenced in the particular child. Turn to the chapter that best describes the identified or suspected disability or condition of the child. Select from the behavioral definitions listed at the beginning of the chapter the statements that appear most descriptive of the child's needs or challenges or appear to be interfering the most with the child's progress along the developmental continuum.

Step Three: Goal Development

The next step in treatment plan development is that of setting broad goals for the resolution of the target problem. These statements need not be crafted in measurable terms but can be global, long-term goals that indicate a desired positive outcome to the treatment procedures. The *Planner* suggests several possible goal statements for each problem, but one statement is all that is required in a treatment plan.

Step Four: Objective Construction

In contrast to long-term goals, objectives must be stated in behaviorally measurable language. It must be clear when the child (or parents) have achieved the objectives; therefore, vague, subjective objectives are not acceptable. Various alternatives are presented to allow construction of a variety of early childhood treatment plan possibilities for the same presenting problem. The early childhood specialist must exercise professional judgment as to which objectives are most appropriate for a given child, along with salient parent input.

Each objective should be developed as a step toward attaining the broad goal. In essence, objectives can be thought of as a series of steps that, when completed, will result in the achievement of the long-term goal. There should be at least two objectives for each problem, but the professional may construct as many as are necessary for goal attainment. Target attainment dates may be listed for each objective. New objectives should be added to the plan as the child's treatment progresses. When all the necessary objectives have been achieved, the child should have resolved the target problem successfully.

Step Five: Intervention Creation

Interventions are the instructional and/or therapeutic actions of the early childhood professional designed to help the child complete the objectives. There should be at least one intervention for every objective. If the child does not accomplish the objective after the initial intervention has been implemented, new interventions should be added to the plan.

Interventions should be selected on the basis of the child's needs and the early childhood specialist's full instructional and/or therapeutic repertoire. *The Early Childhood Education Intervention Treatment Planner* contains interventions from a broad range of approaches, including cognitive, behavioral, pre-academic, motoric, medical, and family-based. Other interventions may be written by a specialist to reflect his/her own training and experience. The addition of new problems, definitions, goals, objectives, and interventions to those found in the *Planner* is encouraged, because doing so adds to the database for future reference and use.

Some suggested interventions listed in the *Planner* refer to specific books or journals where specific methodologies can be located for the specialist to look for a more lengthy explanation or discussion of the intervention. Appendix B contains a full bibliographic reference for the professional, organized by disability or condition. Appendix A offers a bibliographic reference for parents, suggesting reading material that may be helpful to families, referenced by disability or condition.

HOW TO USE THIS PLANNER

The Early Childhood Education Intervention Treatment Planner was developed as a tool to aid early childhood professionals in conjunction with parents in writing an early childhood treatment plan in a rapid manner that is clear, specific, and highly individualized, according to the following progression:

1. Choose one presenting problem/condition (Step One) you have identified through your assessment process. Locate the corresponding page number for that problem/condition in the *Planner*'s table of contents.
2. Select two or three of the listed behavioral definitions (Step Two) and record them in the appropriate section on your treatment plan form. Feel free to add your own defining statement if you determine that the child's behavioral manifestation of the identified problem is not listed.
3. Select one or more long-term goals (Step Three) and again write the selection, exactly as it is written in the *Planner* or in some appropriately modified form, in the corresponding area of your own form.
4. Review the listed objectives for this problem and select the ones that you judge to be clinically indicated for your student (Step Four). Remember, it is recommended that you select at least two objectives for each problem. Add a target date allocated for the attainment of each objective, if necessary.
5. Choose relevant interventions (Step Five). The *Planner* offers suggested interventions related to each objective in the parentheses following the objective statement. But do not limit yourself to those interventions. Just as with definitions, goals, and objectives, there is space allowed for you to enter your own interventions into the *Planner*. This allows you to refer to

these entries when you create a plan around this problem in the future. You may have to assign responsibility to a specific person for implementation of each intervention, dependent upon the team members carrying out the treatment plan.

Congratulations! You should now have a complete, individualized, early childhood treatment plan that is ready for immediate implementation for the child. It should resemble the format of the sample plan that follows on page 9.

A FINAL NOTE

One important aspect of effective treatment planning is that each plan should be highly tailored to the individual child's disability, problems, deficit areas, and/or needs. The child's strengths and weaknesses, unique stressors, social network, family circumstances, and symptom patterns *must* be considered in developing a treatment strategy. Drawing upon our own years of educational and clinical experience, we have put together a variety of treatment choices. These statements can be combined in thousands of permutations to develop detailed treatment plans. Relying on their own good judgment, early childhood professionals can easily select the statements that are appropriate for young children within a specific setting. In addition, we encourage readers to add their own definitions, goals, objectives, and interventions to the existing samples. It is our hope that *The Early Childhood Education Intervention Treatment Planner* will promote effective, creative early childhood treatment planning—a process that will ultimately benefit the child, the team working with the child, the parents, and the greater community.

SAMPLE TREATMENT PLAN

PROBLEM: SCHOOL ENTRY READINESS

Definitions: Has had minimal exposure to pre-academic readiness activities.

Lacks parental involvement with overall development.

Social development has been delayed due to a lack of experiences with peers as a preschooler.

Exhibits a poor self-concept and minimal self-confidence (e.g., withdraws socially, refuses new activities, never volunteers, seldom speaks to adults).

Goals: Achieve enjoyment, confidence, and high self-esteem from approaching and attaining learning tasks.

Participate positively with parents in various pre-academic readiness activities.

Enter kindergarten working toward ongoing success at developmental level of readiness.

OBJECTIVES

1. Parents meet with staff to discuss concerns regarding their child's preparedness for the upcoming kindergarten experience.

2. Increase the frequency of positive social interactions with peers to advance overall social development.

INTERVENTIONS

1. Conduct a meeting with the parents to explore their concerns and the concerns of the staff regarding their child's preparedness for kindergarten; discuss ways they can assist their child in acquiring skills and make their child more prepared to learn.

1. Encourage the parents to enroll their child for more time in the classroom or an alternative setting (e.g., church school, playgroup) to provide their child with more opportunities for social interaction with age peers.

2. Direct a socially adept peer to initiate and maintain social interaction with the child; point out the adept peer's positive skills for

	the child to emulate, reinforcing success immediately as it occurs.
	3. Bring the child into a carefully orchestrated small playgroup supervised by an adult in a private area in the classroom where there is less confusion to allow him/her to practice prosocial behavior with direction (e.g., puppet theater, playhouse, loft area, book corner); reinforce steps toward prosocial behavior.
3. Engage enthusiastically in emerging literacy skills.	1. Reinforce the child for being focused on books (e.g., give verbal praise when the child is looking at a book, when the child is selecting a preferred book, when the child is able to answer simple questions about a story with and without visual prompts).
	2. Create a literacy center in the classroom that allows comfortable places for the child to be involved with a variety of books, a place to listen to books with headphones, a magnetic board with numbers and letters for manipulation by the child, an area devoted to writing with various writing tools, and a place for the child to create his/her own books with adult assistance.
	3. Read to and with the child daily and encourage the parents to do the same at home.
4. Accurately verbalize the letters of the alphabet and improve phonemic awareness skills.	1. Give many opportunities for the child to attain an awareness of the letters of the alphabet (e.g., reading alphabet books, offering alphabet blocks in a play area, having manipulative letters for the child to see, touch, and use for play).

2. Provide phonemic awareness activities on a daily basis (e.g., interacting with the child with books having rhyming and alliteration, playing rhyming games).

5. Attain an awareness of early numeric concepts.

1. Expose the child to sets of objects reinforcing the concepts of more, same as, and less than.

2. Give opportunities for the child to manipulate magnetic numerals for the beginning steps of number recognition as well as teaching simple rote counting; play games such as *Hi Ho Cherry-O* to reinforce early math concepts.

6. Parents seek information regarding the kindergarten program of their child's future school.

1. Arrange for the kindergarten teacher(s) and principal at the local school to meet with the parents to give both the parents and child a tour of the classroom(s) and school; give information about classroom management, the curriculum, the daily schedule, and answer questions from the parents and child.

2. With the parent's permission, exchange information about the child between the classroom personnel and the kindergarten staff.

7. Readily transition into kindergarten with excitement and enjoyment.

1. Encourage the school staff to create a welcoming environment, giving the child a feeling of belonging and the ability to succeed, ensuring a safe learning environment and meeting the basic needs of the child for a strong sense of security for parents and child.

2. If the child incurs difficulty with transition, encourage the kindergarten teacher(s) to schedule a

home visit to talk with parents
and child regarding concerns
and develop a plan for providing
needed changes.

AGGRESSIVE BEHAVIOR

BEHAVIORAL DEFINITIONS

1. Engages in fighting and physical attacks on others, such as hitting, kicking, pinching, and/or biting.
2. Has used an object in an attack that can result in serious harm to others.
3. Steals from others.
4. Destroys belongings of others.
5. Shows cruelty to animals.
6. Exhibits risk-taking behaviors such as running from a parent in public places.
7. Shows an emerging interest in or preoccupation with playing with fire.

—. _____
   _____
—. _____
   _____
—. _____
   _____

LONG-TERM GOALS

1. Terminate all fighting, physical attacks, and violence toward people and animals.
2. End all stealing and destruction of others' personal property.
3. Learn alternative, nonviolent ways to deal with anger and frustration.
4. Demonstrate gains with positive, age-appropriate social development.
5. Parents establish and maintain firm, consistent limits when the child begins to initiate aggressive behaviors.

6. Parents seek counseling resources for changes in the child's behavior, changes in parent style, and/or changes in family dynamics.

—. _____
   _____
   _____

—. _____
   _____
   _____

—. _____
   _____

SHORT-TERM OBJECTIVES

THERAPEUTIC INTERVENTIONS

1. Parents meet with classroom staff to discuss the child's aggressive acts and to determine a plan to address the concerns. (1, 2)

1. With parent permission, contact a school specialist (school psychologist, school social worker, behavioral consultant) to come into the classroom setting to complete observations of the child.

2. Meet with parents to discuss their child's aggressive behaviors in the classroom setting, to gather information as to the child's behavior at home and in other settings, to assist the parents in comprehending the seriousness of their child's actions, and to create a plan with parents to address the concerns.

2. Parents agree to seek a comprehensive evaluation of their child's behaviors and needs with a private clinician. (3)

3. Refer parents to a local agency such as the community mental health center, a child development center, or private psychotherapists specializing in the assessment and treatment of young children.

3. Parents approve the sharing of information acquired through the child's experience in the classroom setting. (4)

4. Obtain parental permission to send observational information from the teacher provider to the clinician, completing the

4. Parents meet with the child's counselor and classroom staff to review evaluation findings. (5)

5. Parents seek a comprehensive evaluation of their child's behaviors and needs, using specialists within the local school agency. (6, 7, 8)

6. Parents collaborate on a Functional Behavioral Analysis and a Positive Behavior Support Plan for their child. (9, 10)

comprehensive evaluation of the child's behavior.

5. Meet with parents and the counselor to discuss evaluation results pertinent to the well-being of the child in the classroom setting.

6. Refer the child to a school psychologist and school social worker to complete a comprehensive psychological and social/emotional/behavioral evaluation (see *Transdisciplinary Play-Based Assessment* by Linder); assess whether this aggressive behavior by the child is of a transient or persistent nature.

7. Refer the parents to a physician or child psychiatrist to medically evaluate the possibility of Attention-Deficit/Hyperactivity Disorder (ADHD) or other psychiatric conditions.

8. Establish a meeting with the parents to review the child's evaluation results; include classroom staff as appropriate.

9. Using evaluation data, a Functional Behavioral Analysis should be developed examining the child's aggressive behavior, antecedents to the behavior, and consequences of the behavior.

10. Develop a Positive Behavior Support Plan targeting acts of aggression occurring in the classroom setting; establish a strong reinforcement system for incompatible, nonaggressive behavior (see *Positive Behavior Support for*

Young Children: A Supplement to Positive Behavior Support for ALL Michigan Students by Mueller and Larson).

7. Parents attend the Individualized Educational Planning Team meeting and endorse the programming and services planned for their child. (11, 12)

11. Convene the Individualized Educational Planning Team meeting; ascertain in collaboration with the parents if the child is eligible for special education and determine the least restrictive environment in terms of programs and/or services.

12. If the frequency, severity, and duration of the child's aggressive behavior warrant it, place the child in a highly specialized classroom with significant behavioral structure and mental health day treatment supports.

8. Significantly decrease episodes of overt aggression. (13, 14, 15, 16)

13. Train staff in the Crisis Prevention de-escalation model to assure that everyone knows appropriate calming and physical management techniques to ensure the safety of the child and adults in an overt, aggressive situation; keep parents fully informed of the need for and use of any physical management of the child (contact Crisis Prevention Institute, Inc., Brookfield, WI, (800) 558-8976).

14. Use time out for the child's aggressive behavior following these guidelines: (1) select a time-out place in an area of the classroom that can be easily monitored; (2) keep an adult with the child as needed; (3) consider use of a "thinking chair" where the child sits for time out; (4) use a formula of 1 minute per age for the time out, not to exceed 5 minutes;

(5) return the child to the time-out place if he/she attempts to leave; (6) keep parents informed of this process.

15. Implement a strong positive reinforcement system involving contingency contracting, where the child earns poker chips, stars, or points that can be exchanged for tangible rewards (e.g., privileges, small toys) for engaging in prosocial, nonaggressive behavior.

16. Make a short list of totally unacceptable behaviors and discuss with parents the use of response cost; that is, the taking away of earned reinforcers and privileges for aggressive acts.

9. Parents learn to provide conditions of safety for their child to help him/her manage aggressive impulses. (3, 17, 18, 19)

3. Refer parents to a local agency such as the community mental health center, a child development center, or private psychotherapists specializing in the assessment and treatment of young children.

17. Provide support to the parents from a school-based specialist (school psychologist, school social worker, behavioral consultant) to help them focus on the physical and psychological safety of their child, so as to decrease his/her aggressive behavior; encourage them to try to reduce any fears of abandonment or danger (see Lieberman and Van Horn entry in *Young Children and Trauma*).

18. In the classroom or daycare setting, create an environment of well-defined safety, comfort, and reassurance.

10. Reduce impulsive aggression through the implementation of a consistent external environment. (20, 21)

11. Use language to express frustration in the place of aggressive behavior. (22, 23, 24)

19. Should issues of child abuse and/or neglect be evident, make an appropriate referral to the local Child Protection Services agency.

20. Designate areas of the classroom/daycare setting for specific activities, such as a play area, art area, or fine motor area; when the child's behavior is incongruent with the expectations of the area, redirect once, and then if he/she is still unable to get back on task, excuse the child to time out for a short period, returning the child to the area with the expectation of working on the appropriate behavior for the area (see *Beyond Time Out* by Stewart).

21. Discuss with the parents the antecedents to the child's angry aggression, teaching them to prevent these by creating a user-friendly environment (e.g., reading the warning signals and taking action—potentially using empathy, logical persuasion, distraction, humor; see *The Explosive Child* by Greene).

22. Assist the child with identifying specific words to express his/her frustration and other angry feelings to bypass an act of aggression; model use of the words and give prompts (e.g., "No hitting, use your words to say how you feel.").

23. Match facial pictures with words to help the child label and categorize his/her feelings; incorporate this process into activities involving other children, emphasizing

various feelings the children identify.

12. Eliminate all stealing and fire-setting behavior. (25, 26, 27)

24. Refer the child to the speech and language pathologist to create a plan for a more nonverbal child to have an effective means of communication (e.g., use of pictures to express needs and wants).

25. Provide close supervision of the child and encourage the parents to do the same, to prevent an opportunity for the child to steal or display fire-setting behavior.

26. Teach fire safety to the large group, potentially with the help of local firefighters, focusing on the targeted child's understanding of fire danger, outcomes of a child's fire, and good and bad fires (see "Three Models of Educational Interventions for Child and Adolescent Firesetters," by Pinsonneault, Richardson, and Pinsonneault in *Handbook on Firesetting in Children and Youth*).

27. When the child steals, have him/her return the object to the owner or appropriate place and give a consequence for the act (e.g., completing required jobs, such as simple cleaning, picking up toys for five days); ask the parents to give the child an opportunity to earn money at home to buy the desired objects.

13. Increase the frequency of positive social interaction, thereby decreasing aggression. (28)

28. Select a specific, structured social skills training program to use with the entire large group, targeting the child of concern, continuing social skill training on the playground and the lunchroom (e.g., *Skillstreaming in Early*

Childhood: Teaching Prosocial Skills to the Preschool and Kindergarten Child by McGinnis and Goldstein).

14. Parents participate in training to improve their child's behaviors and functioning. (29, 30)

29. Encourage the parents to participate in a structured, step-by-step, research-based training where parents are given specific interventions to follow to increase child compliance (e.g., *Defiant Children, Second Edition: A Clinician's Manual for Assessment and Parent Training* by Barkley).

30. Involve parents in working with a school specialist (school psychologist, school social worker, behavioral consultant) in implementing new behavior management techniques with their child (e.g., *1-2-3 Magic: Training Your Preschoolers and Preteens to Do What You Want* by Phelan).

15. Engage in constructive recreational experiences that reduce intensity and frustration. (31, 32)

31. Organize art and music opportunities in the classroom setting that provide relaxation, fun, and success for the child.

32. Encourage the parents to routinely organize special time with their child to engage in leisure, fun activities that are of interest to the child and that strengthen family relationships.

16. Parents express encouragement in their child's progress and feel supported by school/daycare staff. (33)

33. Keep close communication with the parents, discussing successes and concerns of the day or week; per parent request, communicate with outside agencies and professionals to help provide consistency for the child across settings.

—. _____   —. _____
   _____   _____
—. _____   —. _____
   _____   _____
—. _____   —. _____
   _____   _____

ARTICULATION/VOICE CONCERNS

BEHAVIORAL DEFINITIONS

1. Consistently has difficulty with producing and using developmentally expected speech sounds.
2. Demonstrates slower overall speech development.
3. Exhibits deficits in sound production that interfere substantially with communication in the home, preschool, and community.
4. Inaccurate speech patterns (e.g., leaving off the beginnings or endings of words, distorting vowels, leaving out syllables, incorrect sound sequencing) result in significant unintelligibility to those outside the family.
5. Exhibits limited control over movement of the mouth, poor motor planning, tongue thrust, and/or oral-tactile sensitivity (developmental apraxia), which have a negative impact on the quality of speech sounds produced.
6. Speaks with repeated dysfluency (stuttering) as demonstrated by signs of voice tension, a rise in pitch, an increasing length of prolongations, or frequent repetitions interfering with the normal fluency and time patterning of speech.
7. Demonstrates evidence of a voice disorder (e.g., pitch, loudness, vocal quality, and/or resonance) originating from vocal misuse, disease, congenital defects, laryngeal trauma, or neurological disorders.

—. _____
   _____
—. _____
   _____
—. _____
   _____

LONG-TERM GOALS

1. Show significant gains, with mastery of expected speech sounds that are appropriate for age, learning potential, and dialect.
2. Demonstrate substantial progress with intelligibility, improving communication with others in settings outside of the home.
3. Improve oral-motor control, leading to progress with speech clarity.
4. Gain greater fluency in speech.
5. Show progress in overcoming voice anomalies.
6. Parents establish realistic expectations for their child's speech abilities, and work collaboratively with professionals in establishing a quality treatment plan for their child.

—. _____
_____

—. _____
_____

—. _____
_____

SHORT-TERM OBJECTIVES

THERAPEUTIC INTERVENTIONS

1. Parents cooperate, share, and listen to concerns regarding their child's speech. (1)

1. Request a meeting with the parents to discuss concerns regarding their child's speech unintelligibility, dysfluency, or voice quality at home and in the classroom setting.

2. Cooperate with a medical evaluation. (2)

2. Refer the parents to a medical evaluation for their child from a family physician or pediatrician and/or from an otolaryngologist (ear/nose/throat specialist) to identify any organic basis for their child's speech or voice disorder.

3. Participate willingly in a speech evaluation. (3)

3. Refer the parents to the local school agency or a private clinic for access to a speech and language pathologist specializing in the needs of young children.

4. Parents participate in the Individualized Educational Planning Team meeting and accept the recommendations given. (4)

4. Conduct an Individualized Educational Planning Team meeting with the parents present to determine the child's eligibility for special education and the service delivery needs of the child.

5. Cooperate with an occupational therapy evaluation. (5, 6)

5. Refer the parents to an occupational therapist specializing in the needs of young children at the local school agency or in private practice to examine their child's issues with motor planning.

6. Assist the child in the classroom with implementing the occupational therapy treatment plan; encourage the parents to engage in appropriate treatment activities in the home in collaboration with the occupational therapist.

6. Parents take an active role in working positively with their child on articulation issues. (7)

7. Carry out the speech treatment plan with the child in the classroom under the auspices of the speech and language pathologist; collaborate with the parents as they follow through with weekly treatment activities in the home.

7. Correctly produce individual, targeted speech sounds within individual or small group therapy sessions. (8, 9)

8. Facilitate the speech and language pathologist working with the child on targeted sounds using effective methods (e.g., direct instruction activities, sound awareness activities, shaping cues, touch cues; see *Speech Disorders Resource Guide for Preschool Children* by Williams).

9. As the child gains greater accuracy with targeted sound production, integrate his/her practice of sounds into naturalistic and generalized opportunities (e.g., making a craft, planting flowers or seeds, playing a game with emphasis on practice of targeted sounds).

8. Exhibit increased intelligibility and function with greater ease in the pronunciation of sounds, syllables, and words. (10, 11)

10. Facilitate the speech and language pathologist engaging the child in appropriate oral-motor interventions, such as improving oral movement or tactile sensitivity.

11. Support the speech and language pathologist's use of a specific methodology with the child to improve his/her intelligibility, such as the Naturalist Speech Intelligibility Training model (see "A Rationale for Naturalistic Speech Intelligibility Intervention," by Camarata in *Language Intervention: Preschool through the Elementary Years*).

9. Use an alternative communication system effectively as a supplement for communicating wants and needs until intelligibility improves. (12)

12. With support from the speech and language pathologist and collaboration with the parents, assist the child in using a modified sign language method such as Makaton or other visual prompts, such as a picture board.

10. Participate openly and willingly in speech sessions to increase fluency. (13)

13. Support the speech and language pathologist in establishing a warm, caring, and positive relationship with the child through play therapy in preparation for treatment sessions for dysfluency.

11. Parents participate in a contract with the speech and language pathologist to assist their child's dysfluency. (14, 15, 16)

14. Facilitate a 6-week contract between the speech and language pathologist and the parents to promote an appropriate, highly structured parent/child interaction treatment plan to reduce the child's dysfluency (see *Assessment and Therapy for Young Dysfluent Children* by Rustin, Botterill, and Kelman).

15. Assist the parents in identifying the child's fluency disrupters in the home environment; explore

with the parents ways to eliminate or decrease disruptors and ways for parents to assist their child in lessening his/her awareness of the dysfluency (see *Stuttering: An Integrated Approach to Its Nature and Treatment* by Peters and Guitar).

16. Support the speech and language pathologist's goals for the child that emphasize slow versus fast talking, smooth versus bumpy talking, and hard versus easy talking (see *Assessment and Therapy for Young Dysfluent Children* by Rustin, Botterill, and Kelman).

12. Cooperate with the speech and language pathologist in activities selected to improve voice quality. (17, 18)

17. Facilitate the speech and language pathologist working with the child on an individualized voice treatment plan based on medical evaluation outcomes and the child's needs (e.g., elimination of harmful daily vocal habits, learning new techniques without voice strain; see *Communication and Communication Disorders: A Clinical Introduction* by Plante and Beeson).

18. Assign the parents to work at home to modify the environment to try and save voice strain of their child (e.g., keeping a quiet home, rest voice when possible, walking over to speak with a person as opposed to shouting across the room).

13. Parents verbalize an understanding of their child's speech disorder, develop realistic expectations for progress, and seek out positive supportive resources. (19, 20)

19. Conduct a cotreatment model with the speech and language pathologist and staff from the classroom, carrying out workshops on different topics for parents, including speech disorders, to give information and knowledge to parents.

20. Encourage parents to contact organizations or agencies that can provide additional information, such as the American Speech-Language-Hearing Association, 10801 Rockville Pike, Rockville, MD 20852, (800) 498-2071; Stuttering Foundation of America, 3100 Walnut Grove Road, Suite 603, P.O. Box 11749, Memphis, TN 3811-0749.

14. Parents report satisfaction with their child's speech treatment plan and overall progress. (21)

21. Maintain ongoing, frequent contact with the parents, reporting progress and concerns regarding the child's speech needs.

—. _____

_____

—. _____

_____

—. _____

_____

—. _____

_____

—. _____

_____

—. _____

_____

ATTACHMENT CONCERNS

BEHAVIORAL DEFINITIONS

1. Demonstrates a marked deviation or distortion from the general pattern of social relatedness between the child and parents.
2. Fails to initiate or respond to social interactions in an age-appropriate manner (e.g., shows withdrawn behavior or avoidance toward others).
3. Engages in inappropriate and indiscriminate interaction and affection with unfamiliar adults.
4. Fails to show bonding behavior with any caregivers, exhibiting a definite lack of warm and affectionate interactions.
5. Exhibits aggressive behavior toward others, including caregivers.
6. Exhibits excessive dependency and clinging behaviors with caregivers.
7. Has a history of persistent disregard for his/her emotional and physical needs.
8. Has experienced frequent changes in his/her primary caregivers.

—. _____

_____

—. _____

_____

—. _____

_____

LONG-TERM GOALS

1. Show more affection toward home and classroom caregivers.
2. Initiate social connections with others.
3. Decrease the frequency of withdrawn and avoidant behaviors.
4. Show greater self-management and less aggression across social settings.

5. Exhibit increased independence and request assistance from adults in appropriate situations.

—. _____

_____

—. _____

_____

—. _____

_____

SHORT-TERM OBJECTIVES

1. Parents confer with staff regarding behaviors and emotions observed at home and in the classroom. (1, 2, 3)

2. Cooperate with all evaluation tasks. (4)

THERAPEUTIC INTERVENTIONS

1. Classroom staff identify behavioral and emotional concerns regarding the child's daily functioning and create an observational log to document those concerns.

2. Classroom staff make recommendations for a special education consultant (e.g., school psychologist, school social worker) to complete systematic observations and gather data regarding the child's social functioning and needs.

3. Parents and classroom staff discuss potential options as to the need for more extensive psychological evaluation of the child based on the information gathered thus far; refer the parents to a child psychiatrist or psychologist for an in-depth evaluation of their child, if indicated.

4. Complete a psychological/school social work evaluation determining levels of behavioral functioning, cognitive style, intellectual ability, and social needs, using play-based evaluation techniques as appropriate.

3. Parents meet with evaluation staff and collaborate on recommendations by the Individualized Educational Planning Team. (5)

4. Respond to structure, rules, and support by decreasing chaotic, tantrum, disorganized behaviors. (6, 7, 8)

5. Exhibit a significant reduction in the frequency of aggressive behaviors. (9, 10, 11, 12, 13)

5. Prepare evaluation results and conduct an Individualized Educational Planning Team meeting with the primary caregiver, collaborating on determining programming, services, and/or accommodations.

6. Provide considerable routine and a predictable daily schedule in the classroom center; review the daily schedule with the child and give support during transitions from one activity or event to another.

7. Provide structure in the classroom center to assist the child (e.g., a specific place for his/her possessions and centers, organized around themes); specify when and where the child should be in terms of the centers and give guided support with all play sessions.

8. Assist the parents with providing greater structure for the child in the home, supporting the establishment and enforcement of rules, expectations, limit-setting, and natural consequences, balanced with empathy, compassion, warmth, and caring actions.

9. Complete a functional behavioral assessment using data from the psychosocial evaluation and observational information, along with input from parents and classroom staff; outline strategies to use in the classroom, building on the child's strengths, targeting the reduction of aggressive behaviors and reinforcing adaptive replacement behaviors (see *Positive Behavior Support for ALL Michigan Students* [Michigan

Department of Education—
Office of Special Education and
Early Intervention Services]).

10. Instruct parents and selected
classroom staff in techniques of
deep pressure and massage to
assist the child in coping at times
of over-stimulation, anger, and
anxiety (see *The Challenging Child*
by Greenspan).

11. Teach the child abdominal
breathing, muscle contraction,
relaxation, and hand warming
as coping strategies to be used in
times of stress, anxiety, or anger
(see *Infant and Toddler Mental
Health* by Maldonado-Duran).

12. Create a safe plan in collaboration with the family should
the child encounter rage-filled,
aggressive episodes resulting in
safety concerns for self or others (e.g., move the other children
out of the room in a quick and
orderly manner, leaving the
targeted child in the room with a
capable adult who works toward
de-escalation without physical
restraint, if possible, while an ob-
server looks and listens through
the door).

13. Assist the parents with establishing firm boundaries and limits
on the child's expression of anger
at home by maintaining consistency, anticipating and stopping
manipulative behaviors, avoiding
power conflicts, firmly conveying to the child that they will not
allow his/her intense feelings to
become out of control; teach
them effective behavior management techniques.

6. Increase the frequency of social initiation and participation, showing less avoidant, withdrawn, and clinging behaviors. (14, 15, 16)

14. Set up social situations in the classroom in which the child can participate in activities of interest and learn social reciprocity skills (e.g., initiation of play with peers, sharing of toys, selecting others for a game); reinforce the child for positive participation.

15. Slowly establish a routine with the child in which he/she interacts with a selected adult in a close, secure manner (e.g., comes to the adult for help with a specific task or a hug every morning), and then readily transitions to an independent activity without disruption; reinforce the child for his/her ability to engage the adult successfully.

16. Model for the parents and provide the materials (e.g., videotapes, books) for the family to learn techniques of nonintrusive, child-led play techniques to help the child develop social skills and feel like a change agent whose choices and initiatives can make a difference (see *Infancy and Early Childhood: The Practice of Clinical Assessment and Intervention with Emotional and Developmental Challenges* by Greenspan).

7. Classroom staff and family respond consistently and conscientiously to the physical needs of the child. (17, 18, 19, 20)

17. Attempt to ensure that breakfast, lunch, and snack times are delivered as close to the schedule as possible in the classroom center to help the child refrain from over-preoccupation with eating.

18. Provide supervision with food to prevent the child from gulping down, eating excessively, eating inadequately, or hoarding.

19. Monitor the child's toileting and bathroom time; set up a consistent schedule for child's use of the bathroom.

20. Communicate closely with the family in an attempt to establish consistency between the home and classroom center in responding to the child's physical needs.

8. Exhibit patience in waiting for a turn to engage in a desired activity. (21)

21. Establish scenarios where the child must briefly wait for a simple desire (e.g., wait his/her turn to play with a desired toy); give considerable reinforcement for the child's success in waiting without disruptive actions.

9. Verbalize and implement safe behavior rules governing potentially dangerous situations. (22)

22. Teach the child safety rules for potential dangerous situations (e.g., fire hazards, hot stove, traffic, remaining in a seatbelt in a moving vehicle); outline harmful consequences that can occur.

10. Parents seek out a medical examination for their child. (23, 24)

23. Parents seek out medical evaluation, examining any underlying physiological reasons for their child's aggression, poor impulse control, eating, sleeping, and/or toileting dysfunction.

24. Parents share results from the medical evaluation with classroom staff and collaborate on any recommendations.

11. Parents verbalize accurate information regarding child development stages. (25)

25. Teach the family regarding the developmental stages most children evolve through; individualize the discussion to the uniqueness of their child and his/her developmental stages and needs.

12. Parents use a strength-based model to intervene when the child's behavior is maladaptive. (26)

26. Explore with the parents the strengths of the child and of the family unit; encourage them to work through crisis situations

from a strength-based model (e.g., planning which family member is best at talking the child into a de-escalated state, who best communicates with the child psychiatrist, which intervention has the child responded to most successfully in the past, and how can that be altered to be more effective in the future).

13. Provide emotional support to the parents, recognizing their frustration in parenting a detached child. (27, 28)

27. Investigate and refer respite care options that the parents might use for their child.

28. Refer the parents to a mental health clinician specializing in treating young children with attachment concerns.

14. Parents acknowledge that child protective services must be notified by classroom staff. (29)

29. Should neglect or abuse be a function of the child's family experience, a referral to appropriate child protection authorities should be made.

15. Parents verbalize acceptance of their child's needs and resources to provide services to their child. (30)

30. Select a classroom center team member to serve as a primary contact with the family, linking them to any specialists or community agencies to best meet the child's needs (e.g., adoption agency, respite care center, foster care agency, special education classes in school, physician, private psychologist).

16. Parents express confidence in the staff and satisfaction with their child's progress and care in the classroom environment. (31)

31. Establish and maintain frequent, open communication with the family regarding issues, concerns, and successes of their child; select a method of communication most acceptable to the parents (e.g., phone calls, e-mail, communication notebook) and hold periodic face-to-face communication meetings to keep the dialogue open.

ATTENTION/FOCUS

BEHAVIORAL DEFINITIONS

1. Demonstrates less than age-appropriate attention span.
2. Experiences difficulty with keeping attention on tasks or play activities.
3. Does not follow verbal directions consistently.
4. Is easily distracted by extraneous stimuli.
5. Engages in reckless or even dangerous behavior.
6. Frequently shows impulsive actions, such as having difficulty taking turns or interrupting others.
7. Exhibits difficulties in the development of social skills.

—. _____
_____
_____

—. _____
_____
_____

—. _____
_____

LONG-TERM GOALS

1. Gradually increase focus, attention, and concentration.
2. Present with greater self-management, demonstrating decreased impulsiveness and fewer disruptive behaviors.
3. Demonstrate more appropriate social behavior through increased positive interactions with peers.
4. Exhibit the ability to accurately follow one- and two-step directions without prompts.
5. Parents and school staff recognize how difficulties with attention and self-regulation impact the child, and work together to improve the child's overall functioning.

—. _____
    _____

—. _____
    _____

—. _____
    _____

SHORT-TERM OBJECTIVES

1. Parents share with staff their concerns regarding their child's attention and give permission for further assessment, as appropriate. (1, 2, 3, 4)

2. Parents meet with staff to complete an Individualized Education Plan and collaborate on recommendations. (5)

3. Decrease the frequency of high-risk, dangerous, impulsive, or aggressive behaviors. (6, 7, 8, 9)

THERAPEUTIC INTERVENTIONS

1. Organize a meeting with parents to discuss their concerns regarding their child's attention deficits.

2. Review with parents their child's evaluation results and how these findings could be useful in the classroom setting.

3. Suggest to the parents that school personnel with expertise in evaluation (e.g., school psychologist) can be made available to complete further evaluation of their child.

4. Provide a time to meet with parents and school personnel to review results of the additional evaluation information.

5. Hold an Individualized Education Planning meeting, including parents and staff, to determine what, if any, programs or services might be appropriate for the child.

6. Conduct a Functional Behavioral Analysis to ascertain the antecedents occurring prior to the high-risk or aggressive behaviors and the consequences taking place after the behaviors; share this information with parents.

7. Develop with parents and staff a positive reinforcement plan targeting behaviors incompatible with the risk-taking and aggressive behaviors of the child; establish a plan of strong reinforcement of more controlled behavior and use of time out for aggressiveness (e.g., use of a respite area or a thinking chair for time out; see *Positive Behavior Support for ALL Michigan Students: Creating Environments That Assure Learning* [Michigan Department of Education—Office of Special Education and Early Intervention Services]).

8. Maintain communication with the parents about the child's daily success in acquiring one or two target behaviors, as rated by the teacher or caregiver; send this information home and encourage the parents to continue the reinforcement plan.

9. Use physical proximity with the child (e.g., standing close to the child, lightly touching his/her shoulder) and/or a visual signal to improve control over the child's disruptive, impulsive behaviors.

4. Show improved attention with the use of modified auditory and visual stimuli. (10, 11, 12, 13)

10. Create changes in the classroom setting to improve the child's potential for focused attention (e.g., allow access to a minimal number of toys at one time, organize an enclosed place such as a pup tent filled with soft pillows, allow the child to sit in a bean bag chair for quiet activities, at circle time seat the target child next to a quiet, organized child who can provide positive cues for behavior control; see *Pediatric Disorders of Regulation in Affect and Behavior* by DeGangi).

11. Provide auditory inputs that are known by research to improve a child's attention (e.g., play background music such as Mozart, Gregorian chants, music with female vocalists, and relaxing music with environmental sounds; see *Pediatric Disorders of Regulation in Affect and Behavior* by DeGangi).

12. With parent approval, ask the child to wear headphones that muffle noise to reduce auditory distraction and improve attention on certain tasks.

13. Reduce auditory and visual distractions by keeping noise to a minimum, using a circle as the configuration for small group activity, and using physical partitions to block off other environmental stimuli.

5. Increase self-management and attention through the experience of calming activities. (14, 15, 16)

14. Engage the child in goal-directed movement during transition periods of the day in order to enhance focus, expend energy, and minimize the loss of structure (e.g., having the child do some lifting of boxes or furniture to prepare the room for the next activity; see *Pediatric Disorders of Regulation in Affect and Behavior* by DeGangi).

15. Provide body organization, physical stimulation, or energy reduction techniques for the child prior to activities requiring more intensive attention and concentration (e.g., playing with therapy putty, squeezing and pulling resistive toys, burying hands and feet in dried beans or sand, eating a crunchy snack of hard foods; see *Pediatric Disorders of Regulation in Affect and Behavior* by DeGangi).

6. Accurately follow one- and two-step direction. (17, 18, 19)

7. Increase the length of time focusing on and attending to routine activities. (20, 21, 22, 23)

16. Consult with an occupational therapist familiar with the needs of active young children on ways to assist the child with self-regulation and attention through sensory techniques.

17. Model directions, showing the child exactly what he/she is to do, repeating the directions verbally as they are acted out.

18. Teach the child to follow directions by providing him/her verbal repetition of the directions, accompanying each direction with a picture or photograph and placing them in proper sequence.

19. Give immediate positive reinforcement when the child follows a direction accurately.

20. Collect baseline data on the length of time the child is able to attend to one or two routine activities (e.g., circle time, calendar, story time); collect data again after interventions have been implemented for at least a 2-week period.

21. Teach the child the beginning and ending of routine tasks being monitored for attention span techniques (e.g., a time, a mark on a paper every minute, or a picture schedule of events taking place within an activity).

22. Create a chart that visually illustrates improvement of the child's attention to a task; explain the results to the child using the chart.

23. Provide prompt positive reinforcement for any progress the child makes with attending to a routine task.

8. Increase focus and attention through the use of visual and auditory channels of learning. (24, 25, 26, 27)

24. If the child has language capabilities, help him/her use "self-talk" to verbalize the steps necessary to complete a favorite task or activity.

25. Use multisensory approaches to teaching activities to incorporate the child's learning strengths (e.g., emphasize visual strategies if his/her auditory channel is weaker).

26. Instruct the child in task completion using visualization techniques (e.g., show the completed product and then model the step-by-step process to actually make it).

27. Teach the child how to identify the sequence necessary to complete an activity by verbalizing and demonstrating the steps.

9. Increase positive social interactions with peers. (28, 29, 30)

28. Organize a strategically planned play group to take place several times per week where the social engagement is short and very structured, where hands-on materials are available, or where a simple activity is led by an adult (e.g., making peanut butter sandwiches for snack time).

29. During the planned play group, look for teachable moments where the targeted child can learn a prosocial interaction by the adult modeling a positive response to peers; encourage the child to copy this prosocial behavior.

30. Encourage the parents to create play dates in the home for their child with a positive peer and closely monitor the child-to-child interaction, reinforcing prosocial behavior.

10. Parents engage in positive activities that teach their child self-control, sustained attention, and motivation. (31)

31. Encourage the parents to spend several sessions a week engaging in child-centered play; suggest that the child select an interactive and imaginary activity, rather than television, video watching, or board games, where the parent follows the child's lead (see *Infancy and Early Childhood: The Practice of Clinical Assessment and Intervention with Emotional and Developmental Challenges* by Greenspan).

11. Parents respond favorably to their child's progress with attention and associated issues in the classroom setting. (32)

32. Establish routine communication with the parents through their favored choice of communication (e.g., weekly phone calls, e-mail, communication notebook); report to the parents progress, concerns, changes in the child's functioning.

—. _____

_____

—. _____

_____

—. _____

_____

—. _____

_____

—. _____

_____

—. _____

_____

AUTISM

BEHAVIORAL DEFINITIONS

1. Exhibits delayed language acquisition, including limited spoken language.
2. Has no spoken language.
3. Spoken language shows a prominence of echolalia.
4. Demonstrates an inability to initiate social interaction with peers.
5. Social interaction is deficient, including difficulties with basic nonverbal behaviors (e.g., eye contact, facial expressions).
6. Perseverates attention on unusual objects or parts of objects.
7. Has a restricted repertoire of interests and activities, in contrast to age peers, including an inability to engage in representational or dramatic play.
8. Displays repetitive motor movements (e.g., hand flapping, toe-walking and/or rocking).
9. Demonstrates considerable difficulties with change in routine or transition to new activities or places, sometimes resulting in tantrums or even self-injurious acts.

__. _____
   _____
   _____
__. _____
   _____
   _____
__. _____
   _____

LONG-TERM GOALS

1. Acquire some spoken language or learn a basic communication system to express wants and needs.

2. Learn beginning skills of social interaction with peers and adults.
3. Reduce self-stimulating behaviors, extinguish all self-injurious acts, and increase self-regulation.
4. Expand repertoire of interests and activities, decreasing perseverative behaviors.
5. Staff and family develop an understanding of autism and of the child's strengths and deficit areas.

—. _____
   _____
—. _____
   _____
—. _____
   _____

SHORT-TERM OBJECTIVES	THERAPEUTIC INTERVENTIONS
1. The parents meet with staff to discuss concerns regarding their child's functioning in the classroom setting and at home. (1)	1. Establish a conference with the parents to discuss the salient behaviors of their child's functioning at home and in the classroom.
2. The parents agree to the appropriate evaluations to ascertain needs of their child. (2)	2. Refer the parents to the local school for an evaluation for their child or, if parents prefer, provide a list of clinicians who routinely work with special needs children for evaluation in the areas of communication, social/emotional/behavioral functioning, sensory, fine and gross motor skills, and intellectual processing.
3. The parents attend the Individualized Educational Planning Team meeting, accept the outcomes of the evaluations, and agree to the recommendations of the team. (3, 4, 5)	3. Conduct the Multidisciplinary Evaluation Team meeting with parents to discuss the findings of the evaluations of the child's functioning.
	4. Arrange for an Individualized Educational Planning Team meeting with the parents to determine

their child's eligibility for special education programming and/or services and to determine programming options.

5. Refer the parents to a child psychiatrist for further differential diagnosis of an autism spectrum disorder and to provide therapeutic intervention or medication issues.

4. The parents collaborate with staff on a Positive Behavior Support Plan. (6, 7, 8, 9, 10)

6. Using evaluation data, as well as parental and staff observations, develop a Functional Behavioral Analysis, examining the child's behavior, antecedents to behavior, and consequences.

7. Develop a Positive Behavior Support Plan with the parents, targeting the child's aggressive and self-injurious behavior occurring in the classroom setting; establish a strong incentive system for nonaggressive functioning using the child's favored experiences as reinforcers (see *Positive Behavior Support for Young Children: A Supplement to Positive Behavior Support for ALL Michigan Students* by Mueller and Larson).

8. Adopt prevention strategies by manipulating the environment (e.g., changing the setting, changing the activity, changing the participants) to assist the child in not acting or reacting in a volatile manner to a stimulus situation.

9. Carefully scrutinize with the parents the types of interventions to be implemented with the child to prevent or stop self-injurious behavior, adhering to high standards of health, safety, and dignity for the child.

10. Train the staff in the Crisis Prevention Intervention de-escalation model to ensure that all adults in the setting have knowledge of calming and physical management techniques to ensure the safety of the child and adults when the child acts aggressively; keep the parents fully informed of the need for and any use of physical management of the child (obtain information from the Crisis Prevention Institute, Inc., Brookfield, WI, (800) 558-8976).

5. Move beyond the prelinguistic, nonsymbol communication level with the selected mode of communication. (11, 12, 13)

11. Based on the language evaluation, develop a plan with parents and the speech and language pathologist for assisting the child in progressing with communication skills (e.g., teaching the use of picture communication symbols, sign system, switches).

12. Conduct a specialized augmentative evaluation to help determine the type(s) of technology best suited for the child's needs and abilities.

13. Train the staff, parents, and caregivers in how to best support the child with the communication system selected (e.g., train a staff member in sign language, train staff in using the *Picture Exchange Communication System* by Bondy and Frost).

6. Demonstrate gains in acquiring receptive and expressive language skills. (14, 15, 16)

14. Teach basic vocabulary for favorite objects, experiences, and functions in the child's daily environment, moving the child's expressive language from one- to two-word responses; teach one- and two-step directions using pictures to illustrate each step and the desired direction outcome.

15. Move the child along a continuum of progress with his/her echolalia: (1) expand the child's use of echolalia; (2) facilitate the child's echolalia as a communicative tool across people and settings; (3) prompt productive utterances in place of echolalia responses for various purposes in a variety of contexts (see *Autism: Teaching Does Make A Difference* by Scheuermann and Webber).

16. Purposefully engage the child in favored play activities in the classroom and by parents in the home, where joint attention and communication intent can be taught.

7. Adjust more frequently and with greater ease to routine, schedules, and transitions with visual prompts. (17)

17. Create visual prompts to delineate information for the child—to include a picture schedule individualized for the child's day and the use of pictures to designate the child's personal space and belongings in the classroom setting; label centers with pictures displaying their function, and use colored tape or paint to show transition paths to and from routine activities and line-up areas.

8. Increase attention and self-management through engagement in sensory activities. (18, 19)

18. Organize sensory activities individualized for the child that increase self-regulation, producing greater attention, calm demeanor, and more intact behavior (e.g., swinging, jumping on a trampoline, rolling, pushing or pulling heavy loads, sucking and chewing on appropriate food, bouncing on a therapy ball).

19. Seek out a specialist in music therapy to provide a positive sensory experience with music, promoting

9. Engage in beginning social initiation skills with adults and peers. (20, 21, 22)

relaxation, enjoyment, communication, and social relatedness opportunities.

20. Instruct parents on using the "floor time" approach, where the parent follows the child's playful lead, treating every behavior by the child as purposeful, assisting the child with learning to relate to others with warm reciprocity (see "An Integrated Developmental Approach to Interventions for Young Children with Severe Difficulties in Relating and Communicating," by Greenspan and Wieder, in *Zero To Three* [1997, 17:5,18]).

21. Model for the child structured steps to initiating basic social courtesies (e.g., greetings, good-byes, please, thank you); reinforce imitation of these behaviors.

22. Use the guided participation method to assist the child in joining in play with another peer and sharing a toy, making certain to have the play area, materials, carefully-selected peers, and schedule orchestrated for small gains in the child's success (see *Play and Imagination in Children with Autism* by Wolfberg).

10. Respond with gains to a structured, specialized preschool curriculum offering varied and expansive experiential opportunities. (23)

23. Select a structured curriculum for young children on the autism spectrum such as Treatment and Education of Autistic and Related Communication Handicapped Children (TEACCH; Mesibov, Shea, and Schopler), The Denver Model: A Comprehensive, Integrated Educational Approach to Young Children with Autism and Their Families (Ozonoff, Rogers,

and Hendren), or the Social Communication, Emotional Regulation, and Transactional Support Model (SCERTS; Prizant, Wetherby, Rubin, Laurent, and Rydell) to give specialized support to the staff, the child and to his/her family.

11. Demonstrate progress toward independence in performing self-help skills. (24, 25, 26)

24. Assist the child with help as needed to complete daily living tasks such as dressing and undressing, grooming, hygiene, toileting, and self-feeding; reinforce steps toward independent functioning.

25. Consult with the occupational therapist when the child fails to make minimal progress with basic, routine self-care skills practiced in the classroom setting.

26. Enlist the support of a behavioral specialist if the client's toilet training continues to be an issue (considering the child's intellectual functioning and opportunity for practice) to assist the staff and parents with a structured, cohesive plan for success.

12. The parents verbalize a greater understanding of autism and of their child's strengths and needs. (27)

27. Encourage parents to attend an autism parent support group at their local school agency and/or to seek other support (e.g., Autism Society of America, 7910 Woodmont Avenue, Suite 300, Bethesda, MD 20814-3067; Autism-PDD.Net, P.O. Box 1596, Pleasanton, CA 94566; Autism Research Institute, 4182 Adams Avenue, San Diego, CA 92116).

13. The parents express satisfaction with their child's progress in the classroom setting. (28)

28. Create a routine communication plan with the parents (e.g., daily journal, e-mail, weekly phone calls) to encourage open discussions of successes and concerns between home and school.

___. _____   ___. _____
      _____   _____
___. _____   ___. _____
      _____   _____
___. _____   ___. _____
      _____   _____

DEPRESSION

BEHAVIORAL DEFINITIONS

1. Reveals a prevalent pattern of sad or flat affect.
2. Exhibits withdrawn, avoidant, self-isolating behaviors.
3. Demonstrates a lack of interest in play and other age-appropriate activities.
4. Exhibits a tendency for sleep deprivation or engages in excessive sleep.
5. Shows little or no appetite.
6. Exhibits unpredictable changes in mood, with irritability.
7. Frequently complains of somatic problems (e.g., headaches and stomachaches).
8. Exhibits loss of energy, lethargic.

__. _____
   _____
   _____
__. _____
   _____
   _____
__. _____
   _____

LONG-TERM GOALS

1. Elevate mood and show greater energy and enthusiasm for activities.
2. Interact more frequently with peers and adults, showing less avoidant, withdrawn behaviors.
3. Return to more normal sleep and eating patterns and maintain a significant reduction in somatic complaints.
4. Feel less irritable and exhibit more even mood functioning.

5. Participate with a renewed interest in play activities, even initiating play with peers.

—. _____
_____
_____

—. _____
_____
_____

—. _____
_____

SHORT-TERM OBJECTIVES	THERAPEUTIC INTERVENTIONS
1. Parents meet with classroom staff to discuss the child's affect and behavior in the classroom and at home. (1, 2)	1. Share observations with parents regarding the child's apparent sadness, social withdrawal, disinterest in activities, irritability, and other depression indicators.
	2. Obtain permission from the family to have a special education professional (e.g., school psychologist, school social worker) complete observations and report recommendations to the family and staff.
2. Cooperate with all evaluation procedures. (3)	3. Complete a psychosocial evaluation to examine the referral question of early childhood depression to include gathering social, family, medical, and developmental history from the parents and integrating child-focused, play-based evaluation techniques.
3. Parents meet with evaluation staff and collaborate on recommendations by the Multidisciplinary Evaluation Team and Individualized Educational Planning Team as to the child's psychosocial needs. (4)	4. Integrate evaluation results and conduct an Individualized Educational Planning Team meeting with the primary caregiver, collaborating on determining programming, services, and/or accommodations for the child.

4. Parents seek out a medical evaluation from their pediatrician or primary care physician to rule out medical origins for the somatic complaint, eating, and/or sleeping dysfunction. (5, 6)

5. Parents learn about depression, the ramifications for their child, and potential treatment options. (7)

6. Increase the number of positive comments made about self. (8, 9)

5. Refer the parents to the child's physician to obtain a physical examination; ask the family to share medication information with the classroom staff pertinent to the child's somatic complaints, eating, or sleeping dysfunction.

6. Refer the parents to a child psychiatrist to seek a differential diagnosis of depressive disorder and follow the professional recommendations made (e.g., National Mental Health Association at www.nmha.org; *Help Me, I'm Sad* by Fassler and Dumas; *Survival Guide to Childhood Depression* by Dubuque).

7. Give the family information about young children and depression; refer them to a mental health professional in the community who specializes in the treatment of young children with depressive episodes.

8. Use cognitive restructuring with the child to challenge his/her negative comments by gently questioning the child to identify the negative faulty thinking he/she is frequently using; then assist the child with replacing negative thoughts with those emphasizing the positive.

9. Model positive thinking and positive self-talk for the child, by verbalizing positive remarks to the child—then say to the child, "Tell yourself what you are good at doing" . . . or "Tell yourself one thing others like about you" (see *Emotional and Behavioral*

Problems of Young Children by Gimpel and Holland).

7. Use relaxation techniques to improve affect and reduce irritability. (10, 11)

10. Teach the child deep breathing strategies, muscle contraction and relaxation, and guided imagery.

11. Have adults in the classroom frequently model relaxation strategies (e.g., taking deep breaths, relaxing tense muscles) to encourage the child to also use the strategies openly and frequently.

8. Rigorously participate in various physical activities. (12)

12. Create opportunities for the child to engage in physical activities (e.g., riding a tricycle, playing T-ball, swimming) to elevate affect and ensure the child is active.

9. Follow a routine for mealtimes, naptime, snack, and bedtime in the classroom and at home. (13)

13. Attempt to maintain a regular routine for the child in the classroom and at home for mealtimes, naptime, snack, and bedtime, to provide structure and reassurance to the child; minimize change and talk with the child in advance about impending changes.

10. Actively engage in routine pleasurable activities of interest and in new experiences. (14, 15, 16)

14. Schedule the child's favored activities in the classroom and at home at intermittent intervals during the day to offer the child specific times to positively anticipate.

15. Allow the child to bring a favorite object to the classroom (e.g., a special photograph, a note from mom, a lucky penny; something that makes the child feel special and secure).

16. Involve the child in new experiences (e.g., having a friend over,

11. Express feelings openly using pictures to identify those feelings. (17)

12. Eat three meals per day and sleep at normal times. (13, 18, 19)

13. Demonstrate greater animation, social participation, and appreciation. (20, 21, 22)

playing board games, painting, drawing, dancing, singing, or manipulating clay) to stimulate new interests; reinforce the child for participation.

17. Assist the child with identifying his/her feelings by using a feeling chart that shows different faces illustrating different feelings; talk with the child about his/her feelings (see *Emotional and Behavioral Problems of Young Children* by Gimpel and Holland).

13. Attempt to maintain a regular routine for the child in the classroom and at home for mealtimes, naptime, snack, and bedtime, to provide structure and reassurance to the child; minimize change and talk with the child in advance about impending changes.

18. Develop a fun-with-food atmosphere in the classroom where all the children create snacks together and eat together; this can make eating more inviting to the child and clearly a social event.

19. Develop a comfort routine with the child for beginning naptime or for going to bed that involves pleasurable moments for the child (e.g., reading a favorite book to the child, making sure the child has his/her favorite stuffed animal).

20. Direct the staff to provide positive reinforcement to the child (e.g., allowing the child to sit next to special friends during activities, being certain that the child is not in a situation where he/she is

socially isolated, giving frequent verbal praise and encouragement, using external rewards as appropriate, such as sticker charts to reinforce participation; see *Emotional and Behavioral Problems of Young Children* by Gimpel and Holland).

21. Model for the parents and provide the materials (e.g., videotapes, books) for the family to learn techniques of nonintrusive, child-led play techniques to help the child feel like a change agent where choices and initiatives can make a difference (see *Infancy and Early Childhood: The Practice of Clinical Assessment and Intervention with Emotional and Developmental Challenges* by Greenspan).

22. Assign selected staff to participate with the child in the nonintrusive play interaction.

14. Parents express confidence in the staff and satisfaction in their child's progress and care in the classroom environment. (23, 24)

23. Select a classroom team member to serve as a primary contact with the family, obtaining permission for linking to any specialists working with the family to best meet the child's needs (e.g., pediatrician, child psychiatrist, private psychologist).

24. Establish and maintain frequent, open communication with the family regarding issues, concerns, and successes of their child; select a method of communication most acceptable to the parents (e.g., phone calls, e-mail, communication notebook), holding periodic face-to-face communication meetings to keep the dialogue open.

—.   _____   —.   _____

       _____   _____

—.   _____   —.   _____

       _____   _____

—.   _____   —.   _____

       _____   _____

EATING CONCERNS

BEHAVIORAL DEFINITIONS

1. Demonstrates a poor appetite or may be a picky eater, resulting in the consumption of fewer calories and compromised nutrition.
2. Eats far less than is needed, resulting in significantly below-normal weight without any specific medical causality, indicating a failure to thrive condition.
3. Consumes large amounts of food in a compulsive manner, resulting in an obese condition.
4. Engages in a sedentary lifestyle often involving excessive television viewing and computer game playing, contributing to an overweight or obese status.
5. Consumes nonnutritive substances (pica) such as soil, insects, leaves, paint, or stones.
6. Regurgitates and rechews food (rumination), sometimes involving the spitting out of partially chewed food resulting in being at risk for malnutrition, dehydration, and/or dental problems.
7. Exhibits disruptive and oppositional behaviors when in an eating situation (e.g., throwing tantrums, refusing food, refusing to remain at the table).

—. _____

_____

—. _____

_____

—. _____

_____

LONG-TERM GOALS

1. Show substantial improvement in food intake, gaining and maintaining weight within a normal range for age and stature.
2. Demonstrate an increased physical activity level, resulting in a reduction in weight and overall improved health.
3. Terminate consumption of all nonfood items.
4. Resolution of regurgitation, rechewing, and spitting behaviors.
5. Terminate oppositional behaviors and comply with basic eating etiquette.

—. _____
   _____
   _____

—. _____
   _____
   _____

—. _____
   _____

SHORT-TERM OBJECTIVES

1. Parents meet with classroom staff to discuss concerns with the child's eating habits. (1, 2, 3)

THERAPEUTIC INTERVENTIONS

1. Establish a meeting with the parents to discuss with them the staff's concerns with the child's food consumption (too much or too little).

2. Conduct an exchange and gathering of specific information with the family regarding the child's eating habits at home, asking questions such as: What specific problem behaviors does your child show with eating at home? What works successfully to decrease the problems? What food does your child like and dislike? What is a routine mealtime like with your child?

3. Keep a food diary at home and in the classroom to obtain assessment data on how much food the child is consuming and at what times of the day or evening.

2. Cooperate with a comprehensive medical evaluation. (4, 5, 6, 7)

4. Recommend that the parents pursue a comprehensive medical evaluation of the child based on eating concern; ask them to share this information from the medical evaluation, and discuss recommendations to be implemented in the classroom setting.

5. Encourage parents to continue close contact with their physician, pediatrician, or medical specialist in relation to the child's food consumption and growth curve in relation to weight and height.

6. If medication is used to increase the child's weight, the administration and side effects must be discussed with classroom staff.

7. Assess whether the child's motor coordination required for eating is intact; make a referral in collaboration with the parents to an occupational therapist if problems are present.

3. Parents meet with a nutritionist to learn about a balanced diet for their child. (8)

8. Refer the parents to a nutritionist to gather information regarding providing a balanced diet and increasing caloric consumption for their child; identify what nutritional strategies can be used with the child in the classroom setting.

4. Show improvement with appetite, and thus, an increase in food consumption and desired weight gain. (9, 10, 11)

9. Explore with the parents a list of the child's favored foods to offer at snack and mealtimes in the classroom setting.

10. Provide a positive eating environment, making certain the child has appropriate seating, reduced external distractions, and food portions matching the child's age and needs.

11. When the child is a picky eater, maintain a small repertoire of food selections; choose one or two foods a week to introduce to the child and communicate progress with the consumption of these foods to parents.

5. Parents or guardian pursue medical and psychiatric resources should failure to thrive be a suspect condition. (12, 13, 14)

12. Offer to the parents the names of professionals or clinics in the community where a multi-disciplinary team of medical, psychological, and nutritional experts can formally evaluate the child's condition.

13. Obtain information as to the child's psychological evaluation and treatment plan as it applies to the classroom setting; facilitate compliance with the treatment plan within a school setting.

14. If abuse and/or neglect are suspect issues for the child, a referral to the local child protection agency should be made.

6. Consume fewer calories to meet weight loss goals as advised by medical and nutritional professionals. (15, 16, 17)

15. Collaborate with the family on the child's diet and future decreased calorie consumption; identify what nutritional strategies should be used with the child in the classroom setting (e.g., reducing two snacks to one snack per day, substituting low-calorie for high-calorie snacks or meals).

16. Talk with the family about what goals have been set for the child's weight loss; communicate information helpful to parents related to this goal acquisition (e.g., keep a diary of food consumption per day as requested, communicate any new favorite foods as observed at school).

17. Identify with the parents how special events at school (e.g., birthday or holiday celebrations) will be dealt with, to include reducing caloric consumption for the child several days in advance of the event so the child may still participate and maintain weight goal acquisition.

7. Participate with increasing interest and success in a physical activity regimen at school to promote weight loss. (18, 19)

18. Organize increased physical exercise for the child (e.g., bring the child's bike to school, establishing a time for the child to walk a dog, have the class engage in exercise to music, partner the child with a favored older child for a walk).

19. Encourage the family to monitor the child's sedentary activities at home; assist them with identifying alternative activities requiring physical movement and favored by the child.

8. Increase the frequency of appropriate eating behaviors. (20, 21, 22)

20. Model for the child appropriate eating behaviors (e.g., remaining in his/her chair at the table, no food refusal, no throwing of food, no spitting of food, no tantrums, no whining); also, seat the child next to peers with good eating behaviors to serve as models.

21. Pair a food the child enjoys with an unknown food to use favorite foods as a reinforcer and to decrease whining and complaining behaviors about foods placed in front of the child.

22. Look for frequent opportunities to give positive verbal reinforcement when the child is eating appropriately, ignoring negative eating behaviors as much as possible.

9. Decrease significantly disruptive behaviors while eating. (23, 24, 25)

23. Using compliance training, give direct, clear, and concise commands in a positive manner as to the desired behavior (e.g., please sit in your chair at the table while eating; please use your spoon to eat your corn); teach the parents to use such commands at home with praise given for the child's prompt compliance.

24. Follow a specific time-out procedure at eating time for serious disruptive or oppositional behaviors; give a warning and if compliance is not attained, send the child to a time-out chair for an age-appropriate time (see *Assessment and Treatment of Childhood Problems* by Schroeder and Gordon).

25. Monitor the parents' use of time out with the child to help them effectively use these procedures; reinforce success and redirect for failure.

10. Show more normalized acceptance of food and overcoming phobic food behaviors. (26, 27, 28)

26. Discuss with parents the child's food phobic behaviors, such as high sensitivity to odors, flavors, and food consistencies; keep a food and behavior diary for parents to share with their physician (e.g., episodes of gagging, vomiting, apparent fear of swallowing).

27. Obtain information from the parents as to the child's treatment plan at school for the fear-of-food condition as prescribed by the physician, nutritionist, and/or psychiatrist to the family; facilitate compliance with the plan as it applies to the school.

	28. Refer the child and parents to an occupational therapist for the child's sensory defensiveness impacting his/her eating behaviors, for evaluation and recommendations for improvement.
11. End all eating of nonnutritive substances. (29, 30, 31)	29. Discuss with the parents the child's inappropriate eating of nonfood items or the constant regurgitation and rechewing of food; encourage them to seek medical intervention for a potential diagnosis of pica or rumination.
	30. Obtain information from the parents regarding the child's evaluation for pica or rumination (repeated regurgitation and rechewing of food); follow the treatment plan as advised by the physician, psychiatrist, or psychologist, which may include discrimination training (e.g., identifying food from nonfood).
	31. Give the child earned reinforcers for appropriate consumption of food versus nonfood substances.
12. End all rumination behavior. (30, 32)	30. Obtain information from the parents regarding the child's evaluation for pica or rumination (repeated regurgitation and rechewing of food); follow the treatment plan as advised by the physician, psychiatrist, or psychologist, which may include discrimination training (e.g., identifying food from nonfood).
	32. To counteract rumination, serve small portions to the child and inject alternative tasks so the child does not select regurgitation.

13. Parents express satisfaction with their child's progress regarding the targeted food concern. (33)

33. Establish a frequent and comprehensive communication system with the family in addition to a food diary, exchanging salient information between home and school.

—. _____
    _____

—. _____
    _____

—. _____
    _____

—. _____
    _____

—. _____
    _____

—. _____
    _____

ELIMINATION CONCERNS

BEHAVIORAL DEFINITIONS

1. Demonstrates considerable difficulty with achieving consistent toilet training.
2. Has regressed to diurnal enuresis (a repeated pattern of voiding into one's clothes during the day) after toilet training had been consistently achieved.
3. Experiences a lack of daytime bladder control beyond the age of five.
4. Has regressed to nocturnal enuresis (bed-wetting) after a long period of no wetting at night has occurred.
5. Demonstrates nocturnal enuresis beyond the age of seven.
6. Repeatedly passes feces in inappropriate places (e.g., soiling one's clothing) after age four (encopretic).
7. Deliberately smears feces.

—. _____
_____
—. _____
_____
_____
—. _____
_____

LONG-TERM GOALS

1. Parents match the child's developmental level with appropriate toilet training practices to best teach the child bladder and bowel control.
2. Parents practice toilet training in a more positive, flexible, and less rigid manner.
3. Eliminate the diurnal (daytime) episodes of enuresis.

4. End all episodes of encopresis.
5. Stop all smearing of feces.

—. _____
    _____
—. _____
    _____
—. _____
    _____

SHORT-TERM OBJECTIVES

THERAPEUTIC INTERVENTIONS

1. Cooperate with a medical exam in relation to enuretic or encopretic issues. (1, 2)

2. Parents implement consistent and positive toilet training practices for eliminating enuresis. (3, 4, 5)

1. Refer the family to the child's physician to rule out organic or physical causes of their child's enuresis or encopresis; ask the family to share results of the child's medical exam and physician recommendations with the classroom staff.

2. Consult with the family to ensure that medical results and overall maturity of the child indicate he/she is developmentally capable of normal toileting practices, including being both physically and psychologically ready to participate.

3. Discuss with the family the implementation of consistent and positive toilet training practices, with the same procedures being followed at home and in the classroom.

4. Explore with the family any trauma, separation, loss, or rejection experiences that may have led to the child's toileting dysfunction.

5. Refer the family to a private therapist for assistance if rigid, hostile, or critical parental toilet training practices are evident and they are not immediately amenable to change.

3. Parents implement a toileting routine that uses positive reinforcement techniques to teach daytime bladder control. (6, 7, 8, 9)

6. Establish a consistent routine for the child to engage in toileting, obviously varying the schedule when the child indicates a need; implement a similar schedule at home and at school.

7. Have the child practice walking to the bathroom and using the toilet from different places in the home and in the school.

8. Explain to the child's school staff and parents the principles of behavior modification, which uses positive reinforcement of target behaviors; explore and select reinforcers to be used when the child shows evidence of bladder and bowel control.

9. Instruct the parents to conduct checks at specific times during the day to assess if the child is dry and provide the child with a reinforcer when he/she is dry and uses the toilet to eliminate; when the child is wet have him/her assist with cleanup as is age-appropriate.

4. Parents monitor and record the child's progress in learning bladder control. (10, 11)

10. Make the parents and staff aware of the concept that toileting incidents will occur; encourage positive communication and prompts toward the child.

11. Encourage the parents to keep a daytime and/or nighttime wetting log to monitor the child's patterns and progress; complete a

5. Decrease the frequency of nocturnal enuresis. (12, 13, 14)

6. Classroom staff verbalize an understanding of the toileting needs of the child when medical options for treatment of colon impaction are pursued by the family. (15)

7. Cooperate with consuming a high-fiber diet to promote positive bowel elimination practices. (16, 17, 18)

daytime log at the parent's request in the classroom (see *Emotional and Behavioral Problems of Young Children* by Gimpel and Holland).

12. Instruct the parents to strictly limit the child's fluid intake two hours before bedtime and then to check the child for being dry two or three hours after sleep begins; have them gently awaken the dry child to use the toilet and reinforce success.

13. Instruct the parents to immediately bring a dry child to the toilet after awakening in the morning, reinforcing successful use of the toilet to urinate.

14. Explore with the parents their 5-year-old child's success with staying dry at night; encourage the parents to seek a consultation with their family's physician regarding medication use to aid in bladder control and/or the bell and pad/alarm method of awakening the child when wetting begins.

15. Talk with the parents regarding the role of classroom staff in facilitating the toileting needs of the child during the day, when suppositories or enemas are being used at home; communicate these needs to the school staff.

16. Facilitate the school staff in providing the child with snacks and lunches that are commensurate with the physician-recommended diet, most likely to include fruits, vegetables, and grains.

17. Encourage the child to drink plenty of water and fluids during

the day to keep movement through his/her gastrointestinal system, under parent advisement; record fluid intake as needed.

18. Keep the times of eating and the amount of food offered to the child consistent on a daily schedule, which can help keep the natural rhythm of the child's digestive and elimination system effective.

8. Follow an active routine of physical exercise. (19)

19. Organize a daily regimen of physical activities that the child enjoys, builds on his/her strengths, and encourages a regular schedule of elimination.

9. Parents implement consistent and positive toilet training practices for terminating encopresis. (20, 21, 22)

20. Parents and staff work together to establish baseline information as to the child's bowel activity; create a chart so the child is able to see his/her successes.

21. Develop a positive environment at home and school for toilet-sitting times (e.g., giving the child a book, toy, or playing favorite music), matching good feelings with bowel activity.

22. Set up a reinforcement menu where the parents give the child a favorable reward for an appropriate bowel movement at home and at school.

10. Parents respond with acceptance that soiling incidents will occur during the toilet training process and continue to maintain nonpunitive attitudes and actions toward the child. (10, 23, 24, 25)

10. Make the parents and staff aware of the concept that toileting incidents will occur; encourage positive communication and prompts toward the child.

23. Conduct pants checks throughout the day, and when the pants are soiled, assist the child with cleanup in a nonpunitive manner if he/she is unable to do this independently.

24. Teach the parents that a realistic time frame for the child's encopretic behaviors to completely end is 2 to 3 months of treatment with close monitoring.

25. Parents and staff gradually fade incentives for appropriate toileting practices, but reinstate them temporarily if symptoms reappear.

11. Parents read material on the physical issues regarding soiling. (26)

26. Encourage the parents to gain knowledge about soiling by reading information (e.g., "Some Information about Chronic Constipation in Children" by Buchanan and Clayden in *Children Who Soil: Assessment and Treatment*) and reviewing questions with their physician.

12. Parents decrease the child's fearfulness of the toilet using a desensitization process. (27)

27. Collaborate with the family on a desensitization process to include showing photos of a child peacefully remaining on the toilet each time their child enters the bathroom, playing the child's favorite music while he/she is in the bathroom, and giving positive reinforcement (verbal and/or material) for increased time in the bathroom and when elimination successes are achieved.

13. Parents verbalize an understanding of the fact that a referral has been made to a governmental child protection agency. (28)

28. If child abuse is a serious suspicion, notify the local child protection agency.

14. Parents express satisfaction with staff's collaboration and intervention in dealing with their child's elimination issues. (29)

29. Establish a communication system with the family to report on salient events and to maintain the opportunity to exchange information.

___. _____   ___. _____
     _____   _____

___. _____   ___. _____
     _____   _____

___. _____   ___. _____
     _____   _____

EXPRESSIVE LANGUAGE DELAY

BEHAVIORAL DEFINITIONS

1. Expressive language abilities as measured by standardized assessment procedures are substantially below age expectations.
2. Shows evidence of delays in the learning of the sound system (phonological development).
3. Markedly limited expressive vocabulary is significantly below age level.
4. Demonstrates difficulty with learning the grammatical structure (syntax) of language.
5. Exhibits limited social communication due to deficits in expressive language and communicative intent.
6. Engages in a selective mutism that results in failure to speak across most settings.
7. Frustration due to limited or inaccurate oral expression results in a pattern of negative, overt behavior.

—. _____
   _____
   _____
—. _____
   _____
   _____
—. _____
   _____

LONG-TERM GOALS

1. Improve overall expressive language abilities closer to age expectations.
2. Make positive progress with acquisition of phonological skills.
3. Master the beginning skills of correct grammar and sentence structure.
4. Demonstrate improvement with social communication.

5. Resolve issues that are at the origins of selective mutism condition.
6. Extinguish negative behaviors related to frustration over expressive language difficulties.

—. _____
_____
_____

—. _____
_____
_____

—. _____
_____

SHORT-TERM OBJECTIVES

1. Parents meet with staff to discuss concerns regarding their child's language skills. (1)

2. Participate in a comprehensive audiological evaluation. (2)

3. Parents consult with their physician on any potential medical issues interfering with the child's language acquisition. (3, 4)

4. Cooperate with a speech and language evaluation. (5)

THERAPEUTIC INTERVENTIONS

1. Establish a parent/staff meeting to discuss the child's language concerns as identified by classroom staff and the child's parents.

2. Assist the parents with locating an audiologist who routinely works with young children; facilitate a referral and monitor follow-through.

3. Recommend that the parents consult with their child's physician regarding any possible medical issues that may be interfering with language acquisition.

4. Ask the parents to discuss results with the staff from the audiological and medical evaluations, ruling in or out obvious physiological reasons for the child's language delay.

5. Refer the parents to a speech and language pathologist at the local school agency who specializes in evaluating and treating young children, or to a private speech

5. Parents attend the Individualized Educational Planning Team meeting and accept the recommendations. (6)

6. Parents engage in family-centered techniques to assist their child with language development. (7, 8)

7. Demonstrate a reduction in phonological errors. (9)

and language pathologist or clinic with the same expertise.

6. Invite the parents to an Individualized Educational Planning Team meeting to present the evaluation data and determine the child's eligibility for special education programs and/or services.

7. Direct parents on ways they can encourage their child's language development to include: listening to and talking with the child, using enthusiasm and interest; reading to the child every day; avoiding using baby talk; not allowing older siblings to talk for the child; praising any attempts at speaking; and answering questions completely (see *Childhood Speech, Language and Listening Problems* by Hamaguchi).

8. Support the speech and language pathologist in selecting a family-centered intervention program emphasizing the role of the parents in modeling and cuing the child for expressive language; urge the establishment of a caring, supportive environment conducive to the child's ability to take risks (see *Preschool Language Disorders Resource Guide* by Weiss).

9. Facilitate the speech and language pathologist in integrating articulation drills with conversation-based procedures created to bring the child's attention to his/her error pattern; instruct the staff and parents in a simplified method so the child is able to experience language models and practice in natural settings (see

Language Intervention—Preschool Through the Elementary Years by Fey, Windsor, and Warren).

8. Show evidence of an expanding expressive vocabulary. (10, 11, 12)

10. Work with the speech and language pathologist and parents in selecting an individualized set of concepts, words, and messages for the child to begin to vocalize; continue to create words of the week to be emphasized at home and in the classroom setting.

11. With supports from the speech and language pathologist and in collaboration with parents, assist the child in using a modified sign language method such as Makaton or other visual prompts, such as a picture board, to reduce frustration; continue until the child develops a more expanded repertoire of expressive vocabulary.

12. Reorganize the classroom setting to create physical space to maximize language enhancement; develop a set of philosophies that translate into daily language practices, and train staff in language interaction techniques (see "Creating Language-Rich Preschool Classroom Environments" by Justice in *Teaching Exceptional Children,* 2004, 37(2), pp. 36–44).

9. Routinely use two or more words to describe an object, make a request, or give a response to a question. (13, 14, 15, 16)

13. Encourage frequent conversation between the child and an adult about objects and activities to which they are both attending.

14. Assign adults to model, imitate, and expand the child's intended or actual expressive language (e.g., if the child says "no dog," the adult

could say, "you are right, there is no dog, the dog has left").

15. Offer many opportunities for the child to repeat nursery rhymes and finger plays, sing songs, and repeat salient phrases from favorite storybooks that have repetition.

16. Strategically expose the child throughout the day to age peers who are strong language models.

10. Speak in phrases and simple sentences and begin to participate in conversations. (17, 18)

17. Under the supervision of the speech and language pathologist, model with emphasis accurate plurals, verb tenses, pronouns, and appropriate sentence structure.

18. Engage the child in conversational activities that mutually encourage a reciprocal social response (e.g., taking turns with a board game, playing tag).

11. Parents verbalize an understanding of selective mutism and seek assistance for their child. (19, 20, 21)

19. Provide observational data to the speech and language pathologist and the parents as to the time and setting when the child chooses to speak.

20. Refer the parents to a family therapist so that the dynamics or conflicts within the family impacting the child's selective mutism can be identified.

21. Follow the family therapist's recommendations in collaboration with the speech and language pathologist to support the emotional and language needs of the child.

12. Exhibit well-defined progress on goals and objectives in working with the speech and language pathologist. (22)

22. Consult with the parents and the speech and language pathologist to secure information on how the child is progressing with goals

and objectives involving expressive language, and what future interventions should be pursued at home and in the classroom setting for the child to continue to improve.

13. Decrease negative frustration behaviors as a result of additional intervention from a speech therapist and/or behavioral counselor. (23, 24)

23. Should the child struggle with improvement in expressing wants and needs and continue with overt frustration, refer the parents for supplemental speech and language services in a specialized private practice or clinic.

24. Refer the parents to a mental health counselor to obtain behavioral management supports for their child and family; help coordinate speech and language and behavioral supports to best reduce the frustration level of the child at home and in the classroom setting.

14. Parents verbalize an understanding of their child's deficit areas and seek more information to best support their child. (25, 26)

25. Refer the parents to parent workshops focusing on aspects of language development and meaningful ways for parents to assist their child.

26. Provide parents with organizational information such as the American Speech-Language-Hearing Association, 10801 Rockville Pike, Rockville, MD, (800) 498-2071.

15. Parents report satisfaction with their child's progress and with the support from the speech and language pathologist and classroom staff. (27)

27. Communicate frequently and routinely with parents regarding their child's needs, successes, and any concerns or issues that arise.

—. _____

_____

—. _____

_____

___. _____   ___. _____
    _____   _____
___. _____   ___. _____
    _____   _____

GENERALIZED ANXIETY

BEHAVIORAL DEFINITIONS

1. Expresses excessive anxiety, worry, or fear that significantly exceeds what is age-appropriate for the child's stage of development.
2. Complains of frequent physiological symptoms associated with elevated anxiety (e.g., stomachaches, diarrhea, shortness of breath, rapid heartbeat, dizziness).
3. Demonstrates an ongoing elevation of restlessness, motor movement, activity level, muscle stiffness, tension, and/or shakiness.
4. Despite fatigue, displays disturbed sleep patterns involving difficulty falling and remaining asleep and maintaining restful, productive sleep.
5. Focus and attention are below age and development expectations, resulting in a "flight" from one activity to another, with minimal concentration.
6. Gives evidence of a low frustration tolerance through a steady level of agitation and irritability.

—. _____
   _____
—. _____
   _____
   _____
—. _____
   _____

LONG-TERM GOALS

1. Reduce the worry, fear, and anxiety responses to a more manageable level.
2. Decrease the frequency and severity of physical symptoms and exhibit improvement of sleep patterns.

3. Increase attention span, stress tolerance, and achievement motivation in daily classroom functioning.
4. Demonstrate more even mood control with adults and peers, and show greater overall enjoyment of classroom activities.
5. The parents develop a greater understanding of the origins of their child's anxiety and needed treatment procedures.

—. _____
   _____
—. _____
   _____
—. _____
   _____

SHORT-TERM OBJECTIVES

1. Parents meet with school staff to discuss concerns regarding the child's behaviors of anxiety and worry. (1, 2)

2. Participate in evaluation procedures. (3, 4, 5)

THERAPEUTIC INTERVENTIONS

1. Arrange for a collaborative conference between the parents and classroom staff to discuss the child's behaviors of anxiety and worry.

2. Refer the parents to their pediatrician or family physician for a medical evaluation of the child; process the results as they may apply to the child's behaviors in the classroom.

3. Establish a series of observations across settings, (e.g., classroom, home, community) to form the basis for a behavioral assessment of the child's patterns of demonstrating anxiety and worry.

4. Implement components of additional anxiety evaluation techniques, including play therapy, art therapy, or puppet enactment procedures.

5. Provide feedback regarding results of the child's anxiety evaluation to the family.

3. Parents (or primary caregivers) participate with the evaluator(s) in examining origins of their child's anxiety. (6, 7, 8)

6. From the behavioral assessment, identify for the parents (or primary caregivers) the antecedents (events) taking place just prior to the child's anxiety reaction; discuss with the parents potential hypotheses for the increased anxiety.

7. Explore with the parents the family system's underlying conflicts and the presence of fear or anxiety that could be impacting the child.

8. Refer the family to a mental health professional specializing in treating young children with anxiety and worry.

4. Parents engage with staff in creating a positive behavior support plan to reduce their child's anxiety. (9)

9. Using observational and evaluation information, develop a positive behavior support plan with the family, targeting the antecedents that trigger the child's anxiety, and implement consistent positive reinforcement for more adaptive functioning by the child.

5. Implement relaxation techniques to decrease the emotional and physical aspects of anxiety and worry. (10, 11, 12, 13, 14)

10. Use modeling and behavior rehearsal of muscle movement to teach the child relaxation techniques to be implemented several times per week (e.g., "push your shoulders up to your ears and pull your head back down into your shoulders"; see *Clinical Behavior Therapy with Children* by Ollendic and Cerny).

11. Use modeling and behavior rehearsal to teach the child deep breathing exercises as a relaxation technique and as an alternative response to emotional distress.

12. Instruct the child in the proper time to use the relaxation techniques by modeling and incorporating peers to participate.

13. Teach the child the use of positive imagery, where the child is encouraged to recall and verbalize a favorite event or stimulus (e.g., excerpt from a favorite video, a cartoon, a favorite location), to place him/her in a relaxed state at moments of increased anxiety.

14. Engage the child frequently in tactile activities with peers (e.g., playing at the water table or at the sandbox) to reduce stress.

6. Cooperate as an active participant in physical tasks to reduce stress and anxiety. (15, 16, 17)

15. Create a daily regimen of fun-structured physical activities for the child to participate in with peers; at times, provide choices for the child in relation to selection of activities.

16. Monitor the child at unstructured times of the day (e.g., outdoor play) at school to ensure the child does participate in activities which involve at least some movement and physical energy.

17. Collaborate with the family to provide ideas for the child's consistent involvement in developmentally appropriate physical activities when at home.

7. Select favorite peers and/or favorite adults paired with the selection of favorite activities to reduce stress and anxiety. (18, 19)

18. Identify what the child likes to do, what interests him/her, what are his/her strengths and talents; design activities that are based on his/her preferences.

19. Create a time each day when the child can choose from several favorite activities, which are based on his/her preferences, to engage in with a favorite peer or adult.

8. Demonstrate greater competence with age-appropriate

20. Use modeling, puppetry, and individualized and small group

social and problem-solving skills. (20, 21)

instruction to teach basic social skills (e.g., smiling, eye contact, greetings, initiation of simple conversation) to boost the child's self-confidence and to reduce anxiety.

21. Introduce various literature selections to the large group, including the targeted child, that contain themes regarding worry, problem solving and/or self-confidence (e.g., *Wemberly Worried* by Henkes or *Go Away Big Green Monster* by Emberley); lead a simple discussion with the children reiterating ways the characters in the book lessened their worry and/or solved concerns.

9. Exhibit fewer physical symptoms associated with anxiety and worry. (22, 23)

22. Chart the physical symptoms of the child's anxiety (e.g., nausea, diarrhea, shortness of breath), identifying triggers for this distress; use anxiety-reduction techniques (e.g., relaxation strategies, favored activities, physical exercise) as interventions in these crucial time periods to prevent physical symptoms.

23. Consult with the parents concerning the physical symptoms their child continues to exhibit despite classroom interventions, and encourage the parents to implement anxiety-reduction activities in the home setting.

10. Participate in storytelling techniques to describe anxiety-producing situations and healthy reframing of outcomes. (24, 25, 26)

24. Use a narrative approach (White) in which the child writes out the story of his/her anxiety or fear and then acts out the story with the therapist to externalize the issues; work with the child to reach a resolution or develop an effective way to cope with the anxiety or fear.

25. Conduct sessions with a focus on anxiety-producing situations in which techniques of storytelling, drawing pictures, and viewing photographs are used to assist the child in talking about and reducing the level of anxiety or fear.

26. Use a mutual storytelling technique (Gardner) in which the child tells a story about a central character who becomes anxious. The therapist then interprets the story for its underlying meaning and retells the child's story while weaving in healthier adaptations to fear or anxiety and resolution of conflicts.

11. Show increased enjoyment and attention span in classroom activities, as evidenced by actively participating and completing 50 percent of all daily activities. (27, 28)

27. Monitor and gather data after interventions have been implemented to ascertain their effectiveness in increasing the degree of the child's classroom participation and task completion; reinforce his/her success and redirect for failure.

28. Observe the emotional status of the child at several consistent intervals in the day to evaluate his/her affect and to note if there is an increase in enjoyment with as well as engagement in daily classroom activities; reinforce apparent evidence of relaxation and enjoyment.

12. Parents implement basic concepts of acceptance and support with their child to lessen worry and anxiety. (29)

29. Instruct the parents in strategies of acceptance and support that will assist their child in overcoming fear and worry (e.g., being mindful of the child's slow pace of developing a sense of security in new social situations, modeling a positive, non-anxiety social approach, avoiding overprotection,

preparing the child in advance for transitions, asking others to be patient with the child, providing unconditional love and caring; see *Shyness: A Bold New Approach* by Carducci).

13. Parents verbalize constructive ways to respond to the child's anxiety. (30)

30. Work with the parents in family sessions to develop their skills in effectively responding to the child's fears and anxieties with calm confidence, rather than fearful reactivity (e.g., parents remind the child of a time when he/she handled a fearful situation effectively; express confidence in the child's ability to face the fearful situation).

14. Reframe situations that triggered feelings of fear. (31, 32)

31. Counsel the parents to help the child to reframe situations that trigger feelings of fear by discussing events rationally and logically with their child.

32. Use rational emotive techniques to help the child to identify situations that have contributed to fearful feelings and to reevaluate these events in a more realistic and positive manner (see *A New Guide to Rational Living* by Ellis).

15. Implement a routine nightly sleep pattern. (33, 34)

33. Assist the parents in developing a bedtime routine for the child that reduces anxiety and encourages sleep (e.g., taking a bath or shower, playing soft music, reading a story, repeating a positive self-talk phrase, or counting backward until sleep occurs).

34. Counsel the parents to provide the child with an environment that is conducive to peaceful nighttime sleep and to support and/or enforce a bedtime routine.

16. Parents indicate a high level of trust with staff and pleasure with their child's progress. (35, 36)

35. Talk with parents at drop-off and pick-up times as well as during established communication meetings to review concerns and problem-solve viable options for the child's improvement.

36. Designate a staff member to act as a case manager in collaborating with other professionals and agencies who are involved with supporting the child; obtain written parental permission for this communication.

__. _____
    _____
__. _____
    _____
__. _____
    _____

__. _____
    _____
__. _____
    _____
__. _____
    _____

HEARING DEFICITS/DEAFNESS

BEHAVIORAL DEFINITIONS

1. Suffers from a mild (under 40db) to profound (over 91db) hearing loss that interferes with communication.
2. Test results indicate a severe or profound hearing loss that mandates that the auditory channel is not the primary means of speech and language development.
3. The hearing loss or deafness is due to genetics, in utero infections, post-birth disease, trauma, or an unknown cause.
4. Assessment reveals a conductive hearing loss that results in interference of the sound transmission to the inner ear due to difficulties in the outer ear canal or middle ear, and can be improved by medical or surgical intervention.
5. Audiological and medical examination indicates a sensorineural hearing loss that results in impaired functioning of the cochlear or auditory nerve, which can be improved with modern hearing aid devices but not through surgical means.
6. The hearing impairment can be managed through sound amplification techniques (e.g., hearing aids, vibrotactile aids, artificial cochlear).
7. The hearing impairment must be managed through various communication modes, including auditory-verbal, cued speech, oral/aural, total or simultaneous communication, or signed communication.

—. _____

_____

_____

—. _____

_____

_____

—. _____

_____

LONG-TERM GOALS

1. Demonstrate adjustment to technological management strategies (e.g., hearing aids, cochlear implant, other assistive listening devices) put in place to facilitate the highest quality of hearing possible.
2. Show continuing progress with the acquisition of language and communication skills.
3. Develop early auditory skills to maximum potential given the level of hearing impairment.
4. Integrate socially into the classroom center, exhibiting social initiation and social response with peers and adults.
5. Parents work collaboratively with specialists and classroom staff, demonstrating understanding and acceptance of their child's hearing deficits and seeking out resources to support their child's needs.

—. _____
_____
—. _____
_____
—. _____
_____

SHORT-TERM OBJECTIVES

1. Cooperate with an audiological and medical exam. (1)

2. Participate in a speech and language evaluation and overall communication assessment. (2)

3. Parents select the mode of communication best suited for their child to progress with the communication process, given his/her medical, audiological,

THERAPEUTIC INTERVENTIONS

1. Refer the child and family to an audiologist and an otolaryngologist or otologist for audiological and physical evaluation of the inner, middle, and outer ear.

2. Refer the child and family to a speech–language therapist who specializes in young children with hearing loss and to the consultative staff for the hearing impaired available in the local schools.

3. Assist the parents with selecting the mode of communication that would appear to best meet their child's needs (e.g., auditory-oral, total communication, or manual)

and present language development status. (3, 4)

taking into consideration the
child's age and developmental
level as well as his/her level of
hearing loss.

4. Provide the parents with literature
   to review, offer program visitations, arrange consultations with
   educational specialists in hearing
   loss, and provide opportunities
   to speak with other parents of
   hearing impaired or deaf children
   (see *Communication and Communication Disorders* by Plante and
   Beeson).

4. Parents participate in the
   Individualized Educational
   Planning Team meeting and
   collaborate on the recommendations of the team. (5, 6)

5. Meet with the family to obtain
   their input into the evaluation of
   their child's hearing loss and its
   effect on learning potential; interpret evaluation data to them.

6. Organize an Individualized Educational Planning Team meeting
   with parents to discuss available
   programs and services; prioritize
   goals and objectives appropriate
   for the child.

5. Family and classroom staff
   identify through observation
   and interaction with the child
   when the amplification equipment seems to need adjustment,
   and seek assistance from a
   qualified specialist. (7, 8, 9)

7. Assign the school audiologist,
   hearing-impaired teacher consultant, and/or teacher of the
   hearing impaired to monitor
   amplification and other assistive
   devices used by the child to ensure
   proper function.

8. Facilitate the school audiologist, hearing impaired teacher
   consultant, and/or teacher of
   the hearing impaired in providing education to the family and
   appropriate classroom/daycare
   center staff in the basic function
   and operation of amplification
   and other assistive devices for
   awareness purposes.

6. Participate in an instructional process designed to increase intelligible speech production. (10, 11, 12, 13)

9. Arrange for audiological evaluations every 6 to 12 months to provide updated information on the child's hearing loss, monitor the child's hearing devices, and educate the family and classroom staff about these issues.

10. Coordinate the results of the Individualized Educational Plan in matching the selected communication methodology with the program and services that follow that methodology; assist the family with enrollment of the child in the specified program or initiation of appropriate services.

11. Establish a step-by-step instructional plan in the targeted communication mode with the family (e.g., auditory-verbal approach, cued speech, total or simultaneous communication, or signed communication); provide written material to help instruct the family in effective procedures (e.g., *Not Deaf Enough: Raising a Child Who is Hard of Hearing* by Candlish, *For Families: A Guidebook for Helping Your Young Deaf or Hard of Hearing Child Learn to Listen and Communicate* by Schuyler and Sowers, or *Literacy and Your Deaf Child: What Every Parent Should Know* by Stewart and Clarke).

12. Establish a classroom environment that promotes conversation, using facilitative activities and systematic experiences to offer the child many opportunities to develop competency with communication (e.g., prepare the child to answer specific questions, such

as simple items about a story, then call upon the child to respond in front of peers; establish a play group where the child needs to request toys and share toys with others using his/her mode of communication).

13. If a verbal communication mode is selected, model appropriate speech through the amplification system, creating frequent functioning opportunities for the use of beginning speech; give positive reinforcement, encouragement, and feedback to the child for speech use (see *Effectively Educating Students with Hearing Impairments* by Luetke-Stahlman and Luchner).

7. Practice language comprehension strategies demonstrating continuous progress with understanding and mastering language. (14, 15, 16, 17)

14. Support the child's comprehension by using "selective emphasis," that is, targeting key features of what is being communicated and emphasizing those most important points; help the child to identify the most salient elements (see *Hearing Impairment and Language Disorders* by Butler).

15. Select relevant and multiple contexts for teaching vocabulary, where the activities, interactions with peers and adults, and the classroom arrangement are conducive to the child's interests, are meaningful for the child, and have a familiar theme.

16. Implement the use of a curriculum that is targeted for the child with hearing impairments, is developmentally appropriate, offers many hands-on and experienced-based activities, and is tailored

to the child's needs and strengths (see *Mainstreaming Deaf and Hard of Hearing Students* by the National Information Center on Deafness).

17. Organize visual prompts in the child's environment as additional supports to his/her language comprehension and vocabulary development (e.g., label objects in the room using words and a picture depicting the function of the object; provide visual schedules with pictures of the events taking place that day, along with the time of day).

8. Parents implement strategies designed to increase the child's intelligible speech. (18, 19, 20, 21, 22)

18. Teach parents how to implement specific research-based language processing strategies to use with their child, such as frequently using nouns and modifiers in communication (e.g., using specific language with naming objects and using descriptor words to tell about objects in the child's environment, and conveying these words to the child in the child's selected mode of communication; see *The Young Deaf or Hard of Hearing Child: A Family-Centered Approach to Early Education* by Bodner-Johnson and Sass-Lehrer).

19. Instruct parents when the child gives an accurate response or a more lengthy response than normal in his/her mode of communication, to give frequent and enthusiastic affirmative feedback (see *The Young Deaf or Hard of Hearing Child: A Family-Centered Approach to Early Education* by Bodner-Johnson and Sass-Lehrer).

20. Encourage parents to show their child relationships between things and events (e.g., buying tickets provides a seat at a movie or at a musical with favorite cartoon characters; using money allows us to buy things we need and want; see *The Young Deaf or Hard of Hearing Child: A Family-Centered Approach to Early Education* by Bodner-Johnson and Sass-Lehrer).

21. Teach parents that they should give gentle guidance in prompting the child to communicate, but ask rather than tell the child what to do; in this regard, the child has greater opportunity to respond on his/her terms and in his/her mode of communication (see *The Young Deaf or Hard of Hearing Child: A Family-Centered Approach to Early Education* by Bodner-Johnson and Sass-Lehrer).

22. Strongly encourage parents to have the child lead and control the reciprocity of conversation interaction, thereby promoting more communication and initiative on the part of the child (see *The Young Deaf or Hard of Hearing Child: A Family-Centered Approach to Early Education* by Bodner-Johnson and Sass-Lehrer).

9. Follow cues of tactile-kinesthetic sensations to enhance speech and language development. (23)

23. Use touch in various ways to aid the child's development of speech reception and speech production (e.g., feeling the voicing on the chest or pitch on the larynx, feeling air flow for production of certain sounds, associating touch on the finger, palm, or arm for

10. Attend to auditory stimuli when given visual cues or amplified sound. (24, 25, 26)

11. Exhibit positive social skill development and a positive self-identity across settings. (27, 28, 29, 30)

sound's duration or intensity, tapping speech rhythms on the child's wrist or knee (see *Diagnosis and Treatment of Hearing Impairment in Children* by Pappas).

24. Structure the learning environment (classroom and home) with sound treatment for optimum listening by the child (e.g., eliminate competing sounds, establish a reasonable speech-to-noise ratio, use technology to amplify as appropriate).

25. Teach the child how to localize or find different sounds in various environmental settings by cueing listening behaviors with the aid of visual prompts and playing age-appropriate listening games (e.g., pointing to own ear or cupping hand behind own ear when sounds should be listened for).

26. Encourage the family to engage in reading picture books to their child, promoting initiation of listening, vocabulary, and comprehension.

27. Structure classroom activities such as play times to ensure the child is meaningfully engaged and included in activities with peers.

28. Provide modeling of social initiation with peers and guided social interaction, integrating the child with selected peers.

29. Encourage the child to perform tasks independently, as appropriate (e.g., self-care and safety behaviors); give positive reinforcement for success and redirect for failure.

30. Discuss with parents the need for the child to demonstrate appropriate independence and offer suggestions for family outings and activities that reinforce the child's strengths and self-esteem (e.g., if the child enjoys athletics, he/she could participate in a swim class for preschoolers; if the child has a curiosity about animals, family excursions to a zoo or a natural history museum could be helpful).

12. Parents understand and accept their child's hearing loss, seek out supports and resources to meet their child's needs, and work collaboratively with classroom staff in developing a quality treatment plan/program for him/her. (4, 5, 31)

4. Provide the parents with literature to review, offer program visitations, arrange consultations with educational specialists in hearing loss, and provide opportunities to speak with other parents of hearing impaired or deaf children (see *Communication and Communication Disorders* by Plante and Beeson).

5. Meet with the family to obtain their input into the evaluation of their child's hearing loss and its effect on learning potential; interpret evaluation data to them.

31. Provide the parents with information regarding local support groups and national organizations (e.g., Alexander Graham Bell Association for the Deaf and the American Speech-Language-Hearing Association).

13. Parents report satisfaction with their child's program/care and general progress. (32)

32. Classroom staff and special education hearing impaired specialists provide parents with frequent, routine communication updates on their child's progress, needs, and successes.

MEDICALLY FRAGILE

BEHAVIORAL DEFINITIONS

1. Presents with a chronic illness or condition that continuously compromises health or results in acute episodes (e.g., pediatric asthma, type one diabetes, sickle cell anemia, cancer, seizure disorders, HIV/AIDS, juvenile arthritis, cystic fibrosis).
2. Demonstrates compromised cognitive, physical, and/or affective functioning.
3. Interruptions in school or daycare attendance occur as a result of hospitalizations or long-term convalescence at home.
4. Has essential medical needs that require environmental changes in the classroom setting.
5. Demonstrates delays with developmental tasks below learning potential due to weakened tolerance to daily activities.

—. _____
   _____
   _____
—. _____
   _____
   _____
—. _____
   _____

LONG-TERM GOALS

1. Maintain the greatest possible degree of normalcy in the classroom setting.
2. Function commensurate with learning potential in relation to general developmental progress.
3. Parents assist staff in understanding the medical condition of their child, providing information and advocating for health accommodations in the classroom setting.

4. Parents work closely with staff to create a quality and safe experience for their child.

—. _____
_____

—. _____
_____

—. _____
_____

SHORT-TERM OBJECTIVES

1. Parents provide information to classroom staff regarding the child's medical condition. (1)

2. Parents give permission for staff to have access to the child's medical records and treating personnel. (2)

3. Parents meet with classroom personnel to assist with specific health-related plans for the child, including the administration of medications. (3, 4, 5)

THERAPEUTIC INTERVENTIONS

1. Arrange for a consultation with the family to discuss salient issues of the child's health and medical condition.

2. Obtain a release of information from parents for medical personnel to provide pertinent health/medical information regarding the child.

3. Organize pertinent staff members, including a school or public health nurse, to review health issues of the child as they relate to the classroom setting.

4. Facilitate a meeting involving the school or public health nurse, a supervisor or teacher from the school, the child's parents, and medical personnel to create protocols that are needed to meet the daily health care issues of the child.

5. Train the staff responsible for the child in specific techniques required for his/her care (e.g., use of inhaler, testing of blood, giving of insulin, process for feeding tube) prior to the child beginning in

the new setting; encourage strict adherence to matters of confidentiality.

4. Parents cooperate in creating a crisis response plan to address potential life-threatening conditions for their child. (6, 7)

6. Develop emergency protocols for serious medical episodes (e.g., seizures, significant respiratory distress) with parents, the school or public health nurse, and other medical personnel by the family.

7. Share emergency protocols with the local emergency medical response units to apprise them of their potential involvement in the crisis care of the child.

5. Cooperate with evaluations performed by the local school system. (8)

8. Refer the child to the local school system where specialized staff can complete evaluations (e.g., speech and language, psychological, physical and occupational therapy) to ascertain the child's deficit areas and needs, as identified in the Individuals with Disabilities Act (IDEA).

6. Parents agree to the recommendations of the Individualized Educational Planning Team. (9, 10, 11)

9. Arrange for a meeting between the Multidisciplinary Evaluation Team and the parents to review evaluation findings.

10. Conduct an Individualized Educational Planning Team meeting with the parents to determine the child's eligibility for programs and/or services and needed accommodations.

11. Work with the special educators in the classroom setting in carrying out specialized assistance to the child (e.g., the physical therapist consults with staff on the extensiveness of ambulation of a child with muscular dystrophy).

7. Consume designated foods in the classroom setting. (12)

12. Provide the child allowed foods in the correct amount at the designated times, following the dietary

8. Participate in an individualized exercise regimen. (13)

9. Communicate essential needs and desires to the level of potential. (14, 15)

10. Demonstrate progress in performing developmental tasks. (16, 17, 18, 19)

guidelines and restrictions given by the parents and nutritionist.

13. Organize an individualized routine of exercise for the child, involving play activities and peer interaction, following instructions provided by the parents and physical therapist.

14. Promote receptive and expressive language skills, with emphasis on communicating wants and needs, following guidance provided by the speech and language pathologist.

15. Request the assistance of the child's speech and language pathologist in developing a system for communicating health issues (e.g., feeling pain, being wet, feeling sick, needing toileting); educate the staff and family in this communication plan.

16. Offer instructional opportunities to the child in the developmental domains of cognition, language, social, early readiness, and fine and gross motor skills.

17. Monitor the child's progress in the developmental domains, providing additional opportunities and supports in areas where the child is showing little progress.

18. Adjust the child's activity level during periods of stress and/or health deterioration, incorporating rest periods and a shortened day; help the child select less strenuous activities.

19. Explore technology-based educational opportunities for the child that may be an option for

home use (e.g., a computer with instructional software geared for preschoolers, or talking books).

11. Parents seek out or accept emotional support for the stressors in coping with their child's illness. (20, 21)

20. Refer the parents to a private mental health clinician for assistance in establishing coping strategies to deal with the stress of having a chronically ill child.

21. Maintain communication (with parents' permission) with the family's mental health clinician to follow guidelines in providing emotional support to the child and family (e.g., the psychologist encourages hugs and other physical contact while the child with cancer is undergoing tests to see if the disease is in remission).

12. Parents advise classroom staff that their child's condition is worsening. (22, 23)

22. Should the condition of the child become more serious, resulting in greater monitoring and attention, consider the addition of a health-care assistant to meet the chronic and acute medical needs of the child.

23. Provide supportive medical training to the assistant and others involved with the child to assure quality care when the child's physical condition is deteriorating.

13. Parents take an ongoing, active role in clearly communicating any changing needs of their child. (24)

24. As the parents provide information about the child (e.g., placing in writing requests for medical care in the classroom setting, reporting changes in the child's condition, reporting new information regarding the child's medical interventions), communicate this clearly to the staff, if necessary, reporting the daily condition of the child.

14. Parents express satisfaction with their child's adjustment, progress, and care in the classroom setting. (25, 26, 27)

25. Contact the parents when emergencies arise, after implementing the protocol developed for such crises.

26. Maintain contact with the school or public health nurse, who remains a medical liaison to the family and medical personnel treating the child.

27. Initiate contact with the child's parents to assess their satisfaction with the treatment their child is receiving in the classroom setting.

___. _____

_____

___. _____

_____

___. _____

_____

___. _____

_____

___. _____

_____

___. _____

_____

MILD COGNITIVE DELAYS

BEHAVIORAL DEFINITIONS

1. Presents with a delay apparent in intellectual processing, resulting in a lack of early problem-solving, generalization skills, and pre-academic learning.
2. Shows slower acquisition of developmental milestones, including language, motor, and adaptive skills.
3. Exhibits less than age-appropriate ability to attend and maintain focus, resulting in a shortened attention span and lessened concentration.
4. Demonstrates a more passive learning style, exhibiting greater dependence on others to solve problems.
5. Presents with long- and short-term memory deficits.
6. Lacks social initiation and response patterns, resulting in difficulty with social engagement with peers.

—. _____
_____
_____
—. _____
_____
_____
—. _____
_____

LONG-TERM GOALS

1. Show progress with attainment of developmental milestones, including intellectual processing, communication skills, motor skills, attention, and social development.
2. Gain greater independence by beginning to master daily self-care tasks.
3. Exhibit increasing intentionality, becoming less passive, taking more initiative, and showing greater motivation and less dependence on others.

4. Socially integrate with nondisabled, same-aged peers with special education support services are provided as needed.
5. Demonstrate increased self-confidence and enthusiasm for learning, showing an ongoing willingness to try new experiences and challenges.
6. Parents identify their child's strengths and needs and set realistic goals for their child's development.

—. _____
_____
_____

—. _____
_____
_____

—. _____
_____

SHORT-TERM OBJECTIVES

1. Parents share developmental and evaluation information with staff. (1, 2)

2. Parents participate in an Individualized Educational Planning Team meeting. (3)

3. Take a more active role in learning activities, showing greater willingness to

THERAPEUTIC INTERVENTIONS

1. Establish a meeting with parents to discuss their child's strengths, needs, and any special issues regarding the child's placement.

2. Review the evaluation data provided by parents, asking questions and obtaining clarification as to the child's needs, including cognitive ability, fine and gross motor skills, adaptive behavior, and emerging social functioning.

3. Conduct an Individualized Educational Planning Team meeting with classroom staff and the child's parents to ascertain special education programs and/or services needed to assist the child in progressing in deficit areas and provide support to the family.

4. Present toys that are of interest to the child and that require the child to activate them, so he/she

participate in exploration as well as increased independence and motivation. (4, 5, 6)

will learn cause and effect and initiate participation.

5. Create scenarios that allow the child to engage in an enjoyable activity, then stop the activity, requiring the child to reinitiate the activity, thereby reducing passivity (e.g., play a musical game where the music is stopped and the child is responsible for giving a signal to begin the game again).

6. Give the child many opportunities to discover, explore, and practice independence in the classroom environment (e.g., offer a variety of activities the child is able to explore on his/her own where cause and effect can be discovered).

4. Implement problem-solving skills. (7, 8, 9)

7. Set up structured learning situations where the problem to be solved and its solution are presented clearly; then provide the child with a problem and two or three choices to reach solution, giving extensive practice until he/she is successful in independent problem-solving (see *Educating Young Children with Special Needs* by Porter).

8. Teach problem-solving steps to the child with prompts and level of difficulty individualized for him/her, following this process: Ask—What is the problem? What do I want to happen? Is what I'm doing working? What else could I do? Choose what to do and do it (see *Educating Young Children with Special Needs* by Porter).

9. Give the child demonstrations, manual guidance, and frequent

5. Increase verbal response to social initiative by staff and peers. (10, 11, 12, 13)

repetition of directions, instruction, and prompts while he/she is engaged in problem-solving tasks.

10. Work closely with a speech and language pathologist in creating a regimen of language tasks and an environment that contains frequent use of age-appropriate language that engages the child in interaction.

11. Provide ample opportunities with peers for play interaction by the child, where favored toys and activities can stimulate communication.

12. Interact with the child in focused and intentional ways to include modeling, imitating and expanding on the child's communication attempts; engaging the child with an object or task and then talk with him/her about the object or task.

13. Make sure communication with the child is at his/her level, to facilitate participation and comprehension; this may require shortening or simplifying directions or stories to prompt a verbal response.

6. Demonstrate increased attention span. (14, 15, 16)

14. Request a systematic observation from a trained professional at the local public school to ascertain baseline information as to the child's attention span and focus abilities.

15. Develop a positive reinforcement behavior plan using the baseline information to increase the child's ability to attend and focus (e.g., giving the child attention when he/she is engaged, and ignoring off-task behavior).

16. Engage the child in preferred activities with favorite materials, giving the child an immediate participant role and extending the child's focus by asking questions or providing a mild challenge (e.g., "I bet you can put together this puzzle. I will watch you").

7. Demonstrate skills related to short-term memory and the ability to classify. (17, 18)

17. Provide the child with instruction and repetition with skill sets involving likenesses and differences, the ability to classify, the ability to arrange objects and events in order, and understanding space and time (e.g., over, under, today, yesterday).

18. Teach the child memory skills through games and activities (e.g., recalling where toys belong in the classroom, remembering the names of peers and teachers, identifying what object has been taken from a small group of objects).

8. Follow one-step directions with accuracy. (19)

19. Give the child specific one-step directions by moving down to the child's level, looking him/her in the eye, speaking directly in a brief, concise manner, repeating the direction, and using visual prompts as needed.

9. Enjoy exposure to and participation with pre-academic skills. (20, 21)

20. Provide the child with prerequisite experiences to early academics (e.g., left to right sequencing in a picture book, scribbling circles, cutting with scissors, counting objects, engagement in songs, finger plays, and poems).

21. Begin the pre-academic experiences in short time spans of 5 minutes, gradually increasing the time, using familiar materials and pairing the child with a peer who is both competent and sensitive.

10. Demonstrate the ability to complete basic self-care skills. (22, 23)

22. Assist the child with help as needed to complete daily living tasks, such as dressing and undressing, grooming, hygiene, toileting, and self-feeding, as is appropriate for a classroom/daycare setting.

23. Refer the child to an occupational therapist when he/she fails to make minimal progress with basic, routine self-care skills practiced in the classroom setting.

11. Demonstrate improved fine and gross motor skills. (24, 25)

24. Organize a set of developmentally appropriate activities for the child to practice hand skills, grasp development, scissors skills, and prewriting tasks; consult with an occupational therapist for recommendations of appropriate activities and needed individualized adaptations for the child.

25. Consult with a physical therapist in designing a developmentally appropriate gross motor activity set to assist the child in progressing with motor skill development (e.g., climbing, balancing, jumping, hopping, kicking, and throwing balls integrated into simple playground games, dance, and sports).

12. Initiate social interaction and cooperation with same-age peers. (26, 27, 28, 29, 30)

26. Teach the child to move to integrative play by modeling and actually helping the child complete the process of approaching another child, offering a toy, and continuing to share other toys with other children; reduce the number of prompts as the child becomes more independent in his/her play.

27. Look for naturalistic social opportunities where classroom staff are able to organize participation by the targeted child into play activities with accepting peers (e.g., wait for the targeted child to show interest in an activity and then show the child how to play with others, reinforcing peers for their involvement).

28. Build in a prosocial aspect to songs, finger plays, and games, pairing the targeted child for participation with different selected peers in activities (e.g., Hokey Pokey, London Bridge, Simon Says).

29. Organize a short activity (e.g., dramatic play) where the staff introduces the activity, suggests play roles and specific ideas for playing with friends (see "Social Relationships of Children with Disabilities and Their Peers in Inclusive Preschool Classrooms" by Odom, Zercher, Marquart, Li, Sandall, and Wolfberg, in *Widening the Circle: Including Children with Disabilities in Preschool Programs* [Odom, ed.]).

30. Monitor and reinforce the child's positive adjustment in the classroom/ daycare setting, including increased social participation and the ability to follow the schedule and routine.

13. Parents report satisfaction with their child's overall classroom experience and progress. (31)

31. Communicate with the parents on a routine, frequent basis, reporting the child's progress, successes, and concerns; respond to their questions regarding the child's limitations as well as his/her strengths and potential.

14. Parents attend a support group
    of other parents with a special-
    needs child. (32)

32. Refer the parents to a local sup-
    port group for families having
    a member with special needs or
    cognitive challenges

—. _____

—. _____

—. _____

—. _____

—. _____

—. _____

MODERATE/SEVERE
COGNITIVE IMPAIRMENT

BEHAVIORAL DEFINITIONS

1. Lacks overall development in contrast to same-age peers, originating primarily in the cognitive domain and affecting learning capacity.
2. Shows limited acquisition of beginning self-care and daily living skills.
3. Presents with significant deficits in communication skills in both receptive and expressive language-processing skills.
4. Exhibits limited interaction with peers and adults, resulting in impaired social skill development.
5. Demonstrates delays in fine motor, gross motor, and eye-hand coordination skills.

—. _____

_____

—. _____

_____

—. _____

_____

LONG-TERM GOALS

1. Develop communication skills to the level of potential, possibly including the use of an augmentative communication device.
2. Show progress with daily living and functional skills to the level of maximum independence possible.
3. Increase prosocial interactions with peers and adults, diminishing any noncompliant or aggressive behaviors.
4. Respond positively to the developmentally appropriate curriculum to build emerging early academic skills.

5. Parents accept their child's level of learning capacity, establish realistic expectations, and seek out resources to assist their child.

—. _____
   _____
   _____
—. _____
   _____
   _____
—. _____
   _____

SHORT-TERM OBJECTIVES

1. Parents share development and evaluation information with staff. (1, 2, 3)

2. Cooperate with a comprehensive communication evaluation. (4, 5)

THERAPEUTIC INTERVENTIONS

1. Establish an enrollment meeting with parents to discuss their child's needs and placement in the classroom setting.

2. Have parents provide written reports identifying the most recent evaluation information about their child's strengths, deficits, and needs.

3. Refer the family to specialists at the local public school agency for cognitive skill assessments to assist in planning (e.g., curriculum-based measures such as *The Carolina Curriculum for Preschoolers with Special Needs* by Johnson-Martin, Jens, Attermeier, and Hacker).

4. Refer the family for an evaluation of their child by a communication specialist at the local public school agency with expertise in augmentative communication.

5. Integrate the recommendations for augmentative communication devices and strategies into the Individualized Educational Planning process.

3. Parents collaborate with school staff in writing an Individualized Educational Plan for their child. (6)

4. Follow a visual schedule of the day's activities. (7)

5. Engage in an increased level of skill-building. (8, 9)

6. Increase competence in performing basic self-care skills. (10, 11, 12)

6. School officials and classroom staff meet with parents to write an Individualized Educational Plan identifying the specific special education programs, services, and goals to help the child progress in deficit areas.

7. Help the child understand his/her classroom activities during each day by providing a visual schedule and explaining to the child what event will take place next.

8. Create a classroom that offers a room arrangement with a variety of activity possibilities (e.g., a sand and water area, fine motor activity area, block and toy area, quiet book area, dramatic play area).

9. Create interventions that increase the child's activity participation; identify alternatives and modify the environment or activity as needed to eliminate barriers to the child's participation (e.g., individualize the sand and water activities to include play choices at the targeted child's developmental level; see *Teaching Students with Severe Disabilities* by Westling and Fox).

10. Provide frequent opportunities in the child's daily schedule for practice of basic self-help functional skills, with assistance as needed (e.g., hand washing prior to eating and after toileting, taking off and putting on his/her coat and shoes at appropriate times, brushing teeth, combing hair).

11. Plan activities that allow development in daily living skills (e.g., a simple cooking task such as making pudding, where the child pours ingredients in a bowl, stirs with a spoon, and takes turns), with assistance as needed.

12. During free playtime, establish viable choices so the child is able to select a favored activity by vocalizing, pointing, or looking at the choice.

7. Achieve increased independence with toileting behavior. (13, 14, 15, 16)

13. Establish a routine for offering the child bathroom opportunities; offer incentives/reinforcers to the child for demonstrating desired toileting behaviors.

14. Talk with parents to ensure there is no medical basis for any apparent obstacles to toileting for the child.

15. Observe and assess that the child is acquiring the functionality prerequisite to independence with toileting (e.g., being able to get pants down and back up).

16. Enlist the expertise of a behavioral consultant to establish a plan that reinforces independence with toileting and decreases or extinguishes difficulties as is developmentally appropriate for the child's ability level.

8. Improve fine and gross motor skills to the level of potential for age and abilities. (17, 18)

17. Organize a set of developmentally appropriate activities for the child to practice hand skills, grasp development, scissor skills, and prewriting tasks; consult with an occupational therapist for recommendations of appropriate activities and needed

individualized adaptations for the child.

18. Consult with a physical therapist in designing developmentally appropriate gross motor activities for the child; activities could include climbing, balancing, jumping, hopping, kicking, and throwing balls, and could be integrated into simple playground games, dances, and sports.

9. Demonstrate progress in achieving the goals of the Individualized Educational Plan. (19, 20)

19. Modify the curriculum to embed the child's goals from the Individualized Educational Plan into daily activities (e.g., at circle time, integrate the child's goals of matching colors and matching shapes with repetitions of this task offered several times per week; see "Classroom Models of Individualized Instruction" by Horn, Lieber, Sandall, Schwartz, and Wolery, in *Widening the Circle: Including Children with Disabilities in Preschool Programs* [Odom, ed.]).

20. Create an activity matrix that identifies the goals from the Individualized Educational Plan, the classroom activities, and the specific skills to be taught to the child to make instruction easier to deliver (see *Building Blocks for Successful Early Childhood Programs: Strategies for Including All Children* by Sandall et al.).

10. Increase the frequency and quality of social interaction with others. (21, 22, 23)

21. Develop with the communication specialist a set of social responses to allow the child to greet others and respond to simple yes/no questions; work with the family to collaborate on the responses set

so the child is communicating in the same manner at home and the classroom.

22. Plan for the child to participate with strategically selected peers in a dyad or small group social activity (e.g., a game, a music lesson, or eating a snack); plan similar events in the community (e.g., pairing the targeted child with two peers for an excursion to obtain an ice cream treat) where social interaction will more naturally take place.

23. Share with the family ways they can increase their child's social interaction (e.g., teach the family successful ways the child is interacting in the classroom; suggest the child's participation with a family member in church or at a community center with same-age peers).

11. Terminate angry outbursts of temper and make requests calmly. (24)

24. Create a positive behavior support plan targeting tantrum behaviors, extinguishing unreasonable outbursts, and reinforcing calm communication to make wants and needs known.

12. Parents report satisfaction with their child's overall classroom experience and progress. (25)

25. Communicate with the parents on a routine, frequent basis, reporting the child's progress, successes, and concerns; respond to their questions regarding the child's limitations as well as his/her strengths and potential.

13. Parents attend a support group for families with special-needs children. (26)

26. Refer the parents to a local support group for families with a member having special needs or cognitive challenges.

___. _____   ___. _____

     _____   _____

___. _____   ___. _____

     _____   _____

___. _____   ___. _____

     _____   _____

OPPOSITIONAL BEHAVIOR

BEHAVIORAL DEFINITIONS

1. Frequently defies or refuses to comply with requests and rules.
2. Engages in temper tantrums that may include screaming, crying, thrashing, and refusing to move, in defiance of direction or limit-setting from an adult.
3. Consistently displays anger, appearing to maintain a low threshold of tolerance and inflexibility.
4. Often is hostile, negative, and defiant toward adults in authority.
5. Deliberately annoys peers and adults and is easily annoyed by others.
6. Shows an impairment in social skill development.

__. _____

_____

__. _____

_____

__. _____

_____

LONG-TERM GOALS

1. End tantruming behaviors, replacing them with a reasonable response to adult requests.
2. Maintain a more even, calm demeanor, actually enjoying some interactions with peers and adults.
3. Show progress with listening to and obeying requests by adults in authority.
4. Demonstrate gains with positive, age-appropriate social development.

—. _____
_____
—. _____
_____
—. _____
_____

SHORT-TERM OBJECTIVES

1. The parents meet with staff to discuss concerns regarding their child's noncompliant behaviors. (1)

2. The parents consent to a Functional Behavioral Analysis to identify specific issues with their child's behavior. (2, 3)

THERAPEUTIC INTERVENTIONS

1. Meet with the parents to describe behaviors of concern regarding their child and to exchange information with them as to their child's behavior at home.

2. Arrange for a psychologist, social worker, or behavioral specialist from the local school to complete observations of the child and interviews with the parents and teacher/daycare staff; develop a Functional Behavioral Analysis of the child's oppositional behavior, antecedents to the behavior, and consequences of the behavior.

3. Collaborate with the parents using data and information from the Functional Behavioral Analysis to develop a Positive Behavior Support Plan targeting the child's oppositional and defiant behaviors occurring in the classroom setting; establish a strong positive reinforcement system for compliant behaviors (see *Positive Behavior Support for Young Children: A Supplement to Positive Behavior Support for ALL Michigan Students* by Mueller and Larson).

3. Decrease the frequencies of episodes of overt defiance. (4, 5, 6, 7)

4. Select a few essential rules and display them with pictures to convey their meaning, reviewing them frequently with all children; communicate these rules to the parents, asking them to reinforce the importance of the child obeying the rules.

5. Implement a token reinforcement system where the teacher gives the child a poker chip or star on a chart accompanied by brief verbal praise, allowing the child to earn chips or stars to be exchanged at the end of the day for a desired tangible reinforcer (see *Emotional and Behavioral Problems of Young Children* by Gimpel and Holland).

6. Implement a time-out procedure for the child's defiant behavior following these guidelines: (1) select a time-out place in an area of the classroom that can be easily monitored by an adult; (2) consider use of a "thinking chair" where the child sits for the time out; (3) use a formula of 1 minute per age for the time out, not to exceed 5 minutes; (4) return the child to the time out place if he/she attempts to leave; and (5) keep the parents fully informed of this process.

7. Train the staff in the Crisis Prevention de-escalation model to assure that all adults clearly know appropriate calming and physical management techniques in a tantrum situation; keep the parents fully informed of the need for and use of any physical management of their child (Crisis Prevention Institute, Inc., Brookfield, WI, (800) 558-8976).

4. The parents engage in daily communication through home-to-school notes to reduce their child's noncompliance in the classroom setting. (8)

5. Engage in rule-governed games with success and enjoyment. (9, 10)

6. Exhibit the ability to make choices and self-manage without disruptive behaviors. (11, 12)

8. Design a simple, daily home-to-school note system where the child is evaluated by the teacher/childcare provider on one or two targeted behaviors, with the adult sharing with the child positive markings on the note; urge the parent to provide considerable praise and possibly a reinforcer at home for successfully meeting goals in the classroom/daycare setting (see *Emotional and Behavioral Problems of Young Children* by Gimpel and Holland).

9. Teach the child several age-appropriate board games (e.g., *Candyland, Chutes and Ladders,* by Milton Bradley), being certain to instruct the child in the rules of the game; reinforce the importance that he/she follow the rules without disagreement and continuously showcase the enjoyment in playing the game.

10. Instruct a group of children in a structured game including the targeted child; reinforce the enjoyment of the game and the importance of following the rules without disagreement.

11. Routinely give the child two acceptable choices (e.g., You may have milk or juice with your snack; You may play with play-dough or puzzles), leaving the child to understand he/she can have control and make choices without defiance.

12. Implement alternative ways to say no and not be confrontive with the child, such as: substituting yes for no (e.g., "Yes, Susie, we

can have another cookie later"); demonstrating the consequences (e.g., "Look, David, see how sharp the scissors are"); giving the child fantasy when he/she cannot have reality (e.g., "Ian, you wish we could go swimming today in the neighbors' pool, but they are not home"); or giving information (e.g., "We have to clean up the yard before we can go"; see *When "No" Gets You Nowhere: Teaching Your Toddler and Child Self-Control* by Brenner).

7. Make transitions to new activities without resistance. (13, 14)

13. Create a specific schedule using pictures and display it in a highly visible location, reviewing the schedule numerous times throughout the day; when the child does not understand what is expected of him/her, refer the child back to the daily schedule, showing what will take place next.

14. Assist the child with transition to new tasks by making routine references to time and the schedule (e.g., It's almost time, only one more minute until we clean up toys and then it is snack time).

8. Self-manage more frequently with a consistent experience in a defined environment. (15)

15. Designate areas of the classroom/daycare setting for specific activities (e.g., a play area, art area, or fine motor area) to define the environment for the child as it relates to the specific task; when the child's behavior is incongruent with the expectations of the area, redirect once; then, if he/she is still unable to get back on task, excuse the child to time out for a short period, returning the child to the area with the expectation

9. Use emotionally descriptive words and adaptive behaviors to respond to frustrating situations. (16, 17, 18)

16. Follow the principles of the R.E.S.P.E.C.T model: use a Relaxed voice and manner; show Empathy concerning the child's behavior; be Specific in describing the desired behavior; Patiently repeat the directive; Encourage the child; express Confidence that the child will comply; find a balance with closely monitoring the child in a Timely manner, not allowing frustration to escalate beyond a point of recovery (see *Beyond Time Out* by Stewart).

of working on the appropriate behavior for the area (see *Beyond Time Out* by Stewart).

17. Teach the child words to express feelings, so that when a more highly emotional scenario occurs, the child can make an adaptive response instead of noncompliance.

18. Teach the child nonaggressive actions to be implemented in highly emotional scenarios (e.g., teaching the child to put his/her head down, to take several deep breaths, to jump up and down, to move to a safe corner equipped with large pillows); model these actions to allow the child to learn adaptive behaviors in the place of aggression.

10. Implement positive social skills and problem-solving techniques. (19, 20)

19. Select a specific, structured social skills training program to use with the entire large group, targeting the child of concern, continuing social skill training on the playground and the lunchroom (e.g., *Skillstreaming in Early Childhood: Teaching Prosocial Skills to the Preschool and Kindergarten Child* by McGinnis and Goldstein).

20. Teach the child problem-solving skills if he/she has sufficient language processing (both receptive and expressive): identifying what the problem is, brainstorming possible solutions, selecting the best option, and examining how successful the selected option was (see *Emotional and Behavioral Problems of Young Children* by Gimpel and Holland).

11. The parents participate in training to reduce their child's oppositional behaviors. (21, 22, 23)

21. Encourage the parents to participate in a structured, step-by-step, research-based training where parents are given specific interventions to follow to increase child compliance (e.g., *Defiant Children, Second Edition: A Clinician's Manual for Assessment and Parent Training* by Barkley).

22. Involve the parents in working with a school specialist (school psychologist, school social worker, behavioral specialist) in implementing new behavior management techniques with their child (e.g., *1-2-3 Magic: Training Your Preschoolers and Preteens to Do What You Want* by Phelan).

23. Working with a school specialist, assign the parents to read selected chapters on defiant children and choose management techniques they would like to implement (see *The Challenging Child* by Greenspan).

12. The parents seek out a professional mental health clinician to assist their child with compliant behaviors. (24)

24. Encourage the parents to seek psychological or psychiatric support for the child and family; provide a list of several clinicians specializing their practice with the treatment of young children.

13. The parents express encouragement in their child's progress and feel supported by school/daycare staff. (8, 25)

8. Design a simple, daily home-to-school note system where the child is evaluated by the teacher/childcare provider on one or two targeted behaviors, with the adult sharing with the child positive markings on the note; urge the parent to provide considerable praise and possibly a reinforcer at home for successfully meeting goals in the classroom/daycare setting (see *Emotional and Behavioral Problems of Young Children* by Gimpel and Holland).

25. Continue to keep in close communication with the parents on a routine basis as well as when crisis situations arise; plan specific dates throughout the year when communication meetings are held with classroom staff, specialists, and the parents to exchange salient information and to work through concerns.

—. _____

—. _____

—. _____

—. _____

—. _____

—. _____

PHYSICAL IMPAIRMENT

BEHAVIORAL DEFINITIONS

1. Presents with an incurable physical condition, disease, or disorder that limits mobility and movement and distorts posture (e.g., cerebral palsy, muscular dystrophy, spina bifida).
2. Physical impairment is life-threatening and results in a medically fragile condition.
3. Exhibits a compromised state in relation to strength, stamina, and endurance.
4. Demonstrates issues with incontinence and lack of bowel control.
5. Has a need for adaptive equipment (e.g., wheelchair, walker) for mobility.
6. Feels frustrated, angry, and/or depressed due to a lack of ready mobility and independence, as well as needing ongoing assistance from others.

—. _____

_____

—. _____

_____

—. _____

_____

LONG-TERM GOALS

1. Function with the maximum possible mobility and access within the school/daycare setting.
2. Use adaptive equipment to attain the greatest degree of independence possible.
3. Engage routinely in self-care tasks.
4. Self-advocate by communicating wants and needs to caretakers as well as other significant adults and peers.

5. Reduce frustration and show motivation to reach highest potential skill levels.
6. Parents work closely with classroom staff to establish a positive and quality experience for their child.

__. _____
   _____
   _____
__. _____
   _____
__. _____
   _____

SHORT-TERM OBJECTIVES

1. Parents provide initial information regarding the child's condition and give permission for access to the child's medical records. (1, 2)

2. Collaborate with classroom personnel on the development of health-related plans for the child in the classroom setting. (3, 4, 5, 6)

THERAPEUTIC INTERVENTIONS

1. Meet with the parents to discuss salient information as to the child's medical condition and special needs.

2. Obtain a release of information from the parents to access the child's medical information that is pertinent for the classroom staff.

3. Organize a team of staff including a school or public health nurse to review the child's health issues as they relate to the classroom/daycare setting.

4. Facilitate a meeting between the school or public health nurse, parents, medical personnel as designated by the family, and pertinent classroom staff to create protocols necessary for the daily health care issues of the child (e.g., catheterization) and/or medical crisis response plans.

5. Use evaluation information presented by the parents and medical

3. Parents collaborate with classroom staff at the Individualized
Educational Planning Team
meeting to formulate recommendations for the care and
training of the child. (7, 8)

4. Perform self-care tasks as
independently as possible.
(9, 10, 11, 12)

personnel as baseline data in
aligning expectations for the
child.

6. Request written consent from the
parents for additional evaluation
information in specific areas to
meet the needs of the child in the
classroom setting.

7. Discuss evaluation data and
conduct an Individualized Educational Planning Team meeting
to determine special education
eligibility, programming, and/or
services.

8. Through meetings with the
family and inservice, assist all
need-to-know personnel in acquiring insight and knowledge
about salient health and mobility needs of the child; encourage
strict adherence to matters of
confidentiality.

9. Formulate a plan with the
classroom staff, family, and
occupational and/or physical
therapists to identify and teach
targeted simple self-care routines
that the child can fully or partially
engage in (e.g., self-feed process,
toileting, grooming, dressing).

10. Break down each targeted self-
care task into simple behaviors
that are rewardable steps to assist
the child in achieving a successful
outcome (e.g., removal of sock:
push sock down on leg below
ankle, pull sock off over heel, pull
sock completely off).

11. Ask the occupational and/or
physical therapists to recommend
assistive devices and/or technical
aids that may help the child

achieve greater independence with carrying out beginning daily self-care tasks.

12. Create a written procedure for the child's essential and repeated routines to keep staff and family apprised of what procedures are to be used in assisting the child (e.g., a lunch procedure that identifies the goals, seating, equipment, setup, feeding assistance needed, and cleanup; see *Teaching Individuals with Physical and Multiple Disabilities* by Bigge).

5. Cooperate with activities that maximize mobility and physical participation in classroom activities. (13, 14, 15, 16)

13. Collaborate with physical/occupational therapists in evaluating and adapting positioning equipment to ensure the child has maximum safety with appropriate alignment, body support, and seating for classroom needs (e.g., height of a wheelchair to table activities and computer work stations).

14. Request that the physical therapist establish a procedure and train the staff in how to best transfer the child (e.g., out of a wheelchair and onto a toilet), making everyone aware of ways to circumvent difficulties.

15. Organize safe access routines for the child to move about the interior and exterior of the building (e.g., different playrooms, bathroom, lunchroom, playground).

16. Make the physical environment one that encourages and supports exploration, independence, and inclusive practices for the child, using adaptations (e.g., handrails, ramps, roomy work areas, use of standing boards).

6. Engage in fine motor activities with adaptations as needed, gaining proficiency. (17, 18, 19)

7. Implement the use of technology in the daycare/classroom and home setting with appropriate adaptations. (20)

8. Show progress with communication skills. (21, 22)

17. With the assistance of an occupational therapist, adapt toys and other learning materials (e.g., pencils, crayons, puzzle pieces, feeding utensils) with stabilization, control, and grasp to provide the child with maximized fine motor independence (see *Special Education Needs in the Early Years* by Wilson).

18. For the child unable to facilitate any grasp, organize equipment with the help of a therapist so the child is able to use other body parts to draw, color, or write (see *Teaching Individuals with Physical and Multiple Disabilities* by Bigge).

19. Provide switch systems to allow the child to operate equipment ordinarily requiring fine motor skills (e.g., connecting a large switch to a toy to turn it on and off which can be accessed with a hand, head, or foot).

20. Facilitate a match of the child's abilities and needs with appropriate technology (e.g., provide instruction with computer technology to allow the child to use technology in the curriculum and at home; see *Special Education Needs in the Early Years* by Wilson).

21. In conjunction with the speech and language pathologist, reinforce strategies that promote communication skills of the child, including encouraging the child's ability to express wants and needs.

22. Should the child be nonverbal or predominantly nonverbal, follow the direction of the speech and language pathologist in implementing a specific communication system tailored to overcoming this nonverbal deficit (e.g., *Picture Exchange Communication System* by Bondy and Frost).

9. Respond to an augmentative communication system. (23)

23. Implement an augmentative communication system as designed by a specialist that may include the use of low technology devices such as switch interaction or a communication board that speaks when the child touches a picture to assist the child with basic communication needs.

10. Demonstrate a positive self-concept by engaging in activities in areas of strength. (24, 25, 26)

24. Consult the staff and parents to assist the child with establishing a positive self-concept by following these guidelines: (1) help the child understand his/her disability; (2) set and maintain realistic expectations for performance; (3) support and encourage attempts at independence; (4) provide opportunities in areas of strength; (5) provide appropriate discipline (see *The Exceptional Child in the Family* by Ross).

25. Continuously provide activities that allow for the child to build on strengths and competencies, giving feedback with support, encouragement, rewards; keep a visual record to show the child and his/her parents progress.

26. Refer the family to a mental health professional with expertise in disabilities and depression in young children should anger,

11. Parents take an active role in communicating and advocating for the needs of their child to the staff. (27, 28)

12. Parents express satisfaction with their child's overall progress and care in the classroom environment. (29)

—. _____
   _____
—. _____
   _____
—. _____
   _____

frustration, sadness, or negativity become paramount.

27. Encourage and facilitate the parents in communicating their child's needs (e.g., placing in writing requests for medical procedures that need to be implemented during the day, report changes in the child's physical condition, reporting new information from surgeries/medical interventions).

28. Establish the school or public health nurse and the physical and/or occupational therapist as medical and treatment liaisons between the family and the medical personnel treating the child.

29. Establish and maintain frequent, open communication with the parents regarding issues, concerns, and successes of their child; select a method of communication most acceptable to the parents (e.g., home/classroom communication notebook, weekly phone call, e-mail).

—. _____
   _____
—. _____
   _____
—. _____
   _____

RECEPTIVE LANGUAGE DELAY

BEHAVIORAL DEFINITIONS

1. Demonstrates language processing deficits as manifested by difficulty understanding simple words or sentences.
2. Lacks the ability to comprehend the gestures of language used by others.
3. Misses salient auditorily presented information, resulting in problems with following simple directions.
4. Exhibits difficulties with attending to or enjoying auditory tasks such as listening to a story.
5. Deficits in receptive language development and listening skills interfere with acquisition of social and daily living skills.

—. _____
   _____
   _____

—. _____
   _____
   _____

—. _____
   _____

LONG-TERM GOALS

1. Improve receptive language vocabulary closer to age expectations.
2. Gain in the understanding of the language of others, as presented in simple and more complex sentences.
3. Increase the comprehension of the gestures that accompany language (e.g., maintaining eye contact, noticing nonverbal cues).
4. Show good progress with acquisition of listening skills, including following simple oral directions.
5. Parents learn about their child's receptive and listening difficulties, ad-

just to realistic expectations, and seek out resources and supports to assist their child.

—. _____
_____
—. _____
_____
—. _____
_____

SHORT-TERM OBJECTIVES

1. Parents meet with staff to discuss their child's language needs. (1)

2. Participate in a comprehensive audiological evaluation. (2)

3. Cooperate with a speech and language evaluation. (3)

4. Parents attend the Individualized Educational Planning Team meeting and accept the recommendations. (4)

THERAPEUTIC INTERVENTIONS

1. Establish a meeting with the parents to discuss concerns with the child's language, giving examples of deficits noted in the classroom setting and soliciting examples from the home setting.

2. Assist the parents with locating an audiologist for their child who routinely works with young children; facilitate a referral for an evaluation and monitor for follow-through.

3. Refer the parents to a speech and language pathologist at the local school agency who specializes in evaluating and treating young children or to a private speech and language pathologist or clinic with the same expertise.

4. Invite the parents to an Individualized Educational Planning meeting to present the evaluation data and determine the child's eligibility for special education programs and/or services.

5. Demonstrate an increase in receptive vocabulary. (5, 6, 7, 8)

5. Systematically introduce new vocabulary words each week to the child, using visual prompts (e.g., objects, pictures) to show meaning; use the words in different settings and situations (e.g., games, projects, music).

6. Involve the child in various activities designed to teach and reinforce the new vocabulary (e.g., putting together a simple book or photo album).

7. Use concise language when speaking to the child—being specific about what you want him/her to understand.

8. Role-play targeted action words with the child, pairing a verb with a familiar noun the child already knows (e.g., The cat climbs the tree).

6. Parents engage in activities at home to increase their child's receptive vocabulary. (9, 10, 11)

9. Encourage the parents to talk frequently with their child at home, explaining concepts and answering questions.

10. Collaborate with the parents on focusing on new words each week so the same words are being emphasized to the child at home and in the classroom setting.

11. Urge the parents to read daily to their child, discussing the pictures and pointing to objects or characters and asking their child questions such as: What is this? or Who is this? or Is this a coat or a sweater?

7. Expand skills of comprehension from words to sentences. (12)

12. Read simple sentences aloud and have the child match a picture to the meaning; create a sentence and assist the child with putting

8. Accurately identify sounds and their sources, improving auditory attention. (13, 14)

9. Show attention to the cues for listening. (15)

10. Demonstrate 80 percent accuracy in following one- and two-step verbal directions. (16, 17, 18)

together photos to create the sentence in pictures.

13. Play listening games such as *Soundtracks* (Living & Learning, 3195 Wilson Dr., N.W., Grand Rapids, MI 49544) where the child listens to a tape with other children, identifies sounds, and points to a picture of what produced the sound on a card in front of them.

14. Create sounds for the child to identify as he/she concentrates with eyes closed (e.g., water running, door shutting); have the child show what caused the sound if he/she is unable to say it (see *Listening* by White).

15. Teach the child to make eye contact with the person speaking and attend to the verbal prompts for listening (e.g., "Listen carefully," "I want you to listen," "Please listen to what I would like you to do"); give the child many opportunities to positively practice this skill.

16. Give the child a visual cue while verbalizing a direction to him/her, such as showing him/her a picture card depicting the request; assist the child with following through on the direction and give reinforcement for accurate compliance.

17. State a simple direction to the child using familiar vocabulary for the child and ask him/her to repeat the direction before beginning the task.

11. Accurately answer questions
    that reflect story comprehen-
    sion. (19, 20, 21)

12. Demonstrate improved test
    scores after using listening
    technology methods. (22, 23)

18. Provide frequent opportunities
    for the child to follow a direction,
    increasing to a two-step direction
    when the child is ready.

19. Read aloud to the child an age-
    appropriate picture book daily
    and encourage parents to also
    read to their young child every
    day; ask questions of the child
    that only require him/her to
    point to a picture to provide the
    answer.

20. During and after a story is being
    read, ask the child for information
    (e.g., request information that can
    readily be answered by the child
    using the pictures from the story;
    then ask questions that require se-
    quencing [What do you think the
    dog will do next?]; train parents to
    engage their child in story reading
    in the same manner).

21. Assist the child with using his/her
    prior knowledge to comprehend
    a story line (e.g., when reading a
    story about a cat, engage the child
    in a discussion about cats, show-
    ing pictures of different types of
    cats and cats involved in different
    settings or activities).

22. Collect baseline data on the
    child's listening skills by giving
    a simple listening pretest to the
    child, in which he/she is required
    to answer a few simple questions
    about a story that has been read
    and/or follow a two-step verbal
    direction.

23. Introduce the child to technology
    such as an FM system or an audi-
    tory training device; after a

13. Exhibit well-defined progress on goals and objectives in working with the speech and language pathologist. (24, 25)

14. Parents verbalize an understanding of their child's deficit areas and seek resources to support their child. (26)

15. Parents report satisfaction with their child's progress and with the support from the speech and language pathologist and classroom staff. (27)

month of frequent use, repeat the earlier test procedure to ascertain the effectiveness of the technology in aiding the child's listening abilities.

24. Arrange for the speech and language pathologist to meet with the child on a routine, scheduled basis, as determined by the Individualized Educational Planning team in collaboration with parents.

25. Consult with parents and the speech and language pathologist to secure information on how the child is progressing with goals and objectives involving receptive language development and listening skills, and what future interventions should be pursued at home and in the classroom setting for the child to continue to improve.

26. Give the parents a list of speech and language pathologists in private practice or in clinics specializing in treatment of young children for supplementing current treatment; provide parents with organizational information such as the American Speech-Language-Hearing Association, 10801 Rockville Pike, Rockville, MD 20852, (800) 498-2071.

27. Communicate frequently and routinely with parents regarding their child's needs, successes, and any concerns or issues that arise.

___. _____   ___. _____
    _____   _____

___. _____   ___. _____
    _____   _____

___. _____   ___. _____
    _____   _____

SCHOOL ENTRY READINESS

BEHAVIORAL DEFINITIONS

1. Displays low motivation with acquiring new skills.
2. Has had minimal exposure to pre-academic readiness activities.
3. Lacks parental involvement with overall development.
4. Has a history of inadequate physical activity that has interfered with normal growth and development.
5. Health, acuity, and nutrition issues are largely unsupervised by parents.
6. Social development has been delayed due to a lack of experience with peers as a preschooler.
7. Exhibits a poor self-concept and minimal self-confidence (e.g., withdraws socially, refuses new activities, never volunteers, seldom speaks to adults).

—. _____
   _____
—. _____
   _____
—. _____
   _____

LONG-TERM GOALS

1. Achieve enjoyment, confidence, and high self-esteem from approaching and attaining learning tasks.
2. Participate positively with parents in various pre-academic readiness activities.
3. Increase physical activity and balanced nutrition important to brain and body growth and development.
4. Enjoy time with age peers in playgroups, preschool, daycare, church,

school, and so on, prior to kindergarten for progress with social development.

5. Enter kindergarten working toward ongoing success at developmental level of readiness.

—. _____

   _____

—. _____

   _____

—. _____

   _____

SHORT-TERM OBJECTIVES

THERAPEUTIC INTERVENTIONS

1. Parents meet with staff to discuss concerns regarding their child's preparedness for the upcoming kindergarten experience. (1)

1. Conduct a meeting with the parents to explore their concerns and the concerns of the staff regarding their child's preparedness for kindergarten; discuss ways they can assist their child in acquiring skills and make their child more prepared to learn.

2. Parents seek an updated medical evaluation for their child. (2)

2. Provide parents with a list of pediatricians, family practice physicians, and clinics as potential referral sources; recommend they take their child for a medical evaluation to rule out any organic basis for the child's learning issues.

3. Parents pursue acuity screenings for their child to ensure that vision and hearing is intact for school. (3)

3. Provide parents with options where they may obtain a screening for vision and hearing for their child (e.g., local public health department).

4. Show improvement in gross motor skills, compliance, enjoyment, and progress with engaging in a routine physical exercise and activity program. (4, 5, 6)

4. Ask the parents to share information from their child's medical evaluation; collaborate with the parents and a physical education teacher or physical therapist to develop a physical activity/gross

motor program individualized for the child.

5. Create a schedule for the child and his/her peers to routinely engage in physical activities.

6. Establish with the physical education teacher or physical therapist an evaluation schedule, at which time the child's overall physical activity status is conveyed to parents and the staff.

5. Exhibit gains in fine motor skills. (7, 8)

7. Engage the child with his/her peers in an array of fine motor activities such as drawing, painting, sewing cards, cutting and stringing beads; provide guidance and reinforcement.

8. Consult with an occupational therapist for guidance in aiding the child with building fine motor skills.

6. Increase the frequency of positive social interactions with peers to advance overall social development. (9, 10, 11, 12)

9. Encourage the parents to enroll their child for more time in the classroom or an alternative setting (e.g., church school, playgroup) to provide their child with more opportunities for social interaction with age peers.

10. Direct a socially adept peer to initiate and maintain social interaction with the child; point out the adept peer's positive skills for the child to emulate, reinforcing success immediately as it occurs.

11. Engage the child in entry dialogue to assist him/her with learning how to enter a playgroup (e.g., "Let's listen to what they're doing here. What are they playing? What could you do to help with that?"; see "Social Acceptance: Strategies

Children Use and How Teachers Can Help Children Learn Them" by Hazen, Black, and Fleming-Johnson in *Young Children,* 1984, September, pp. 26–36).

12. Bring the child into a carefully orchestrated small playgroup supervised by an adult in a private area in the classroom where there is less confusion, to allow him/her to practice prosocial behavior with direction (e.g., puppet theater, playhouse, loft area, book corner); reinforce steps toward prosocial behavior.

7. Respond more skillfully with active listening and auditory attention. (13, 14, 15, 16)

13. Teach the child listening skills through: (1) talking with the child, describing objects, events, and how things look, sound, and feel, using many adjectives; (2) give simple one- and two-step directions without visual prompts; (3) explain steps in a sequence to the child when completing a task together; suggest these listening ideas to parents for home use.

14. Teach the child to attend to sounds and conversations in the classroom; create scenarios where joint attention occurs between an adult and the child while engaging in the same activity (e.g., the child looks at the book while listening to the adult read).

15. Consider the use of a sound field amplification system in the classroom to improve listening skills of the target child and all children in the setting.

16. Create a listening center where the child can sit with a small group of

8. Demonstrate greater proficiency with visual skill development. (17)

9. Enjoy embedded literacy opportunities. (18, 19, 20)

10. Engage enthusiastically in emerging literacy skills. (21, 22, 23)

peers and listen with headphones to stories and music for enjoyment.

17. Encourage eye-hand coordination and visual skill activities, such as playing with Legos, telling stories to the child that promote visualization in his/her mind, having treasure hunts in the classroom or on the playground using maps, promoting puzzles, board games, and drawing; teach parents to engage in similar activities at home.

18. Display signs and labels that have a purpose in the classroom and that will be frequently visible to the child (e.g., classroom activity areas, directions for hand washing, menu for the week).

19. Place books and magazines not only in the reading corner, but make them a part of activity centers (e.g., magazines and telephone books in the dramatic play area, books about color and shapes in the art area, a lunch menu with forms for restaurant orders in the play kitchen area; see *Building Blocks for Teaching Preschoolers with Special Needs* by Sandall and Schwartz).

20. Use games for the child to practice prereading skills, such as *What's That Sound?* or *Original Memory* by Milton Bradley.

21. Reinforce the child for being focused on books (e.g., give verbal praise when the child is looking at a book, when the child is selecting a preferred book, when the child

is able to answer simple questions about a story with and without visual prompts).

22. Create a literacy center in the classroom that allows comfortable places for the child to be involved with a variety of books, a place to listen to books with headphones, a magnetic board with numbers and letters for manipulation by the child, an area devoted to writing (with various writing tools), and a place for the child to create his/her own books, with adult assistance.

23. Read to and with the child daily and encourage the parents to do the same at home.

11. Accurately verbalize the letters of the alphabet and improve phonemic awareness skills. (24, 25)

24. Give many opportunities for the child to attain an awareness of the letters of the alphabet (e.g., reading alphabet books, offering alphabet blocks in a play area, having manipulative letters for the child to see, touch, and use for play).

25. Provide phonemic awareness activities on a daily basis (e.g., interacting with the child with books having rhyming and alliteration, playing rhyming games).

12. Attain an awareness of early numeric concepts. (26, 27)

26. Expose the child to sets of objects reinforcing the concepts of more, same as, and less than.

27. Give opportunities for the child to manipulate magnetic numerals for the beginning steps of number recognition as well as teaching simple rote counting; play games such as *Hi Ho Cherry-O* by Parker Brothers to reinforce early math concepts.

13. Parents seek information regarding the kindergarten program of their child's future school. (28, 29)

28. Arrange for the kindergarten teacher(s) and principal at the local school to meet with the parents to give both the parents and child a tour of the classroom(s) and school; give information about classroom management, the curriculum, the daily schedule, and answer questions from the parents and child.

29. With the parent's permission, exchange information about the child between the classroom personnel and the kindergarten staff.

14. Readily transition into kindergarten with excitement and enjoyment. (30, 31)

30. Encourage the school staff to create a welcoming environment, giving the child a feeling of belonging and the ability to succeed, ensuring a safe learning environment and meeting the basic needs of the child for a strong sense of security for parents and child.

31. If the child incurs difficulty with transition, encourage the kindergarten teacher(s) to schedule a home visit to talk with parents and child regarding concerns and to develop a plan for providing needed changes.

15. Parents continue their positive involvement and advocacy with their child's learning and overall educational programming and progress. (32, 33)

32. Encourage the kindergarten teacher(s) to develop a routine communication exchange with the parents to address issues and concerns, as well as successes.

33. Facilitate the kindergarten teacher(s), along with support staff (e.g., school counselor, school social worker, or school psychologist), in offering workshops throughout the school year on topics of interest to parents,

reinforcing the concept of parents as teachers and as partners with the school.

___. _____   ___. _____
   _____   _____

___. _____   ___. _____
   _____   _____

___. _____   ___. _____
   _____   _____

SENSORY INTEGRATION NEEDS

BEHAVIORAL DEFINITIONS

1. Has difficulty processing tactile, vestibular, and/or proprioceptive sensory information.
2. Is overreactive to touch (hypersensitive).
3. Is underresponsive to touch (hyposensitive).
4. Exhibits poor tactile discrimination.
5. Lacks body awareness, showing a delay with gross and fine motor skills, impacting progress with daily living skills.
6. Struggles with motor planning and visual perception skills.
7. Demonstrates dysfunction with social interaction (e.g., withdrawal, over-reaction, flight, refusal).
8. Exhibits deficits in balance, as well as general muscle coordination.

—. _____
   _____
   _____
—. _____
   _____
   _____
—. _____
   _____

LONG-TERM GOALS

1. Show responsiveness to touch that is closer to normal limits.
2. Demonstrate improvement in body awareness and overall visual and tactile processing.
3. Show social skill functioning closer to age appropriate level.
4. Achieve greater self-regulation in daily living skills, attention, and personal interaction.

5. Demonstrate progress with motor skills, balance, and general coordination.

6. The parents demonstrate an understanding of their child's sensory processing deficits and how this impacts functioning.

—. _____

_____

—. _____

_____

—. _____

_____

SHORT-TERM OBJECTIVES	THERAPEUTIC INTERVENTIONS
1. Parents meet with classroom staff to discuss their child's sensory processing difficulties. (1, 2)	1. Meet with the parents to discuss concerns about their child's functioning in the classroom setting and at home.
	2. Solicit agreement from the parents that they will record data regarding their child's problematic sensory-related behaviors at home (e.g., date, time, and circumstances over a week's time); staff will do the same in the classroom setting.
2. Parents seek evaluations to assess the specific needs of their child. (3, 4, 5, 6)	3. Encourage the parents, as appropriate, to pursue a medical evaluation for their child with the family physician or pediatrician to provide information as to the child's physical status.
	4. Refer the parents to an occupational therapist (in private practice or within the school system) familiar with sensory integration issues in young children to obtain an evaluation of their child.

3. Parents participate in an Individualized Educational Planning Team meeting, agreeing to the recommendations for services for their child. (7)

4. Show improvement in self-feeding behavior. (8, 9)

5. Demonstrate age-appropriate toileting behavior. (10)

5. Refer the parents to a speech and language pathologist (in private practice or within the local school system) to obtain an evaluation of their child.

6. Refer the parents to a vision professional specializing in the evaluation of young children to rule out vision needs as an issue with the child's dysfunction.

7. Conduct an Individualized Educational Planning Team meeting with parents and appropriate staff to consider the outcome of the evaluations, to integrate the recommendations, and to determine the child's eligibility for special education programs and/or services.

8. Assist the child in the classroom setting and at home with organizing mealtime and snack time (e.g., ensure the chair and table height meet the child's needs, with feet on the floor; offer a variety of foods with different textures, such as crunchy, smooth, lumpy, chewy; give the child a straw to use with drinks; work with the child in using utensils with greater ease and versatility).

9. Give portions of food to the child appropriate for his/her size, weight, and age; encourage and reinforce his/her feeding skills.

10. Monitor the child's bladder and bowel functioning, offering routine and frequent bathroom times, and communicating with the parents regarding chronic wetting or constipation issues.

6. Go to sleep at times designated without significant resistance. (11, 12)

11. Keep a routine for nap time, giving a prompt that nap time is beginning soon; make the sleeping area comfortable and quiet and consider a sleeping bag for the child.

12. Encourage the parents to establish and maintain a bedtime routine, to be certain their child's nightwear is comfortable commensurate with the child's tactile style, and to ensure the bed surface is smooth without bumps.

7. Increase independence in dressing self. (13, 14)

13. Teach the child basic zipping, buttoning, fastening, and shoelacing skills; encourage the child to dress him/herself as independently as possible, gradually reducing assistance.

14. Create a center for all the children that focuses on fine motor dressing skills (e.g., play make-believe Shoe Store, where the children take turns being a customer and a salesperson, allowing considerable practice with lacing or tying shoes; see *The Out-of-Sync Child* by Kranowitz).

8. Demonstrate increased acceptance of bathing, tooth brushing, and hair grooming. (15, 16, 17, 18)

15. Suggest to the parents that they allow the child to make choices about what to wear from two comfortable selections, encouraging the child to dress him/herself as independently as possible while they gradually reduce assistance; use highly-motivating clothes, place large hooks in salient places so he/she can hang up his/her own routinely-used clothes and lay out clothes the night before.

16. Discuss strategies with parents for their child's bathing experience, such as scrubbing the child with firm, downward strokes and using a large tightly wrapped bath towel for pressure; allow the child to help regulate the water temperature, and provide different toys, soaps, and scrubbers for texture, scent, and fun experiences (see *The Out-of-Sync Child* by Kranowitz).

17. Solicit strategies from the speech and language pathologist or occupational therapist that will allow cooperation from the child with tooth brushing, in light of his/her tactile tolerance issues.

18. Reduce the child's reactivity to hair grooming by creating a Beauty/Barber Shop in the classroom, using combs, brushes, and an assortment of hair accessories, with children pretending to be the customer and the stylist (see *The Out-of-Sync Child* by Kranowitz).

9. Participate in sensory activities designed to increase alertness, self-regulation, and relaxation. (19, 20, 21, 22, 23)

19. Working closely with an occupational therapist, organize a balanced array of sensory activities designed to increase the functional skill level and focus of the child.

20. Facilitate sensory activities that increase the child's alertness (e.g., jumping on a trampoline, bouncing on a therapy ball, crunching on hard foods such as apples and pretzels).

21. Organize sensory activities that increase the child's ability to self-regulate (e.g., the pushing or

pulling of heavy objects [with supervision], having the child be upside down).

22. Implement sensory activities that calm the child (e.g., rocking or swinging slowly in a back and forth movement, having the child suck on a frozen treat or a spoonful of peanut butter).

23. Review the goals with parents and the occupational therapist, thereby assisting the child in deficit sensory areas (e.g., improvement of tactile discrimination and defensiveness, body awareness, coordination and balance, motor planning, eye-hand coordination, and visual perception).

10. The parents facilitate the child's participation in sensory activities at home. (24, 25)

24. Facilitate a collaborative relationship between the occupational therapist and parents, to instruct them in activities for their child at home; encourage parents to keep a log of the home activities and to share this log at future meetings.

25. Request from the occupational therapist that he/she talk about the child's difficulties with parents and classroom staff, modify the child's activities and sensory diet experiences as needed, and serve as an advocate for the child in explaining his/her behaviors and needs.

11. Increase the frequency of positive interactions with peers and adults. (26, 27, 28)

26. Provide the child with modeling of prosocial behaviors (both verbal and nonverbal) by a peer, by a supervising adult, by puppetry, and through exposure to videotaped scenes of appropriate

behavior (see "A Social Skills Program for Developmentally Delayed Preschoolers" by Matson, Fee, Coe, and Smith in *Child and Family Behavior Therapy,* 1991, 20, pp. 227–242).

27. Bring the child into a carefully orchestrated small play group supervised by an adult in a private area in the classroom, where there is less confusion, to allow him/her to practice prosocial behavior (e.g., puppet theater, playhouse, loft area, book corner).

28. Teach the parents techniques to use at home to increase the child's prosocial behavior and decrease or extinguish undesirable interfering behavior (e.g., praising prosocial behavior as it occurs naturally at home, modeling prosocial behavior toward peers and encouraging the child to mimic the behavior, interrupting social conflict and suggesting alternative prosocial responses).

12. Respond with less sensory reactivity due to salient and well-planned classroom interventions. (29)

29. Simplify the classroom setting through reducing tactile, visual, auditory, olfactory, and movement distractions as much as is viable, providing comfortable and practical seating, keeping a daily routine with planned transitions between activities, simplifying instructions, giving positive choices, creating an understanding classroom climate, and speaking in a quiet and low-pitched voice.

13. Increase the ability to regulate and cope with emotions. (30, 31, 32)

30. At home and in the daycare setting, anticipate situations where too much stimulation is evident

and remove the child to a quiet, calm environment.

31. Give the child words that describe emotions he/she is feeling, giving reassurance and empathy; reinforce expression of emotions in a controlled manner.

32. Provide structure and set limits on the child, using natural consequences, instruction, and time away in place of punishment for unregulated emotional expression.

14. Parents seek appropriate resources for treatment of their child's depression and/or behavioral challenges. (33)

33. Should the child's frustration not lessen or actually increase, and depression and/or serious self-regulation dysfunction continue to compromise the child's behavior despite interventions, assist the parents with identifying potential psychotherapists who understand sensory issues and who routinely work with young children and their families.

15. Parents communicate effectively with staff and express satisfaction with their child's progress. (34, 35)

34. Establish a routine preferred system of communication with parents (e.g., e-mail, weekly phone call, daily journal), talking with parents regarding the child's strengths, successes, needs, and crisis scenarios.

35. Provide the parents with organizational contacts that may enhance their knowledge of their child's sensory integration issues (e.g., the Sensory Integration Education & Research Foundation, P.O. Box 30, Camp Hill, PA, 17001-0030, (717) 731-8672, www.sierf .org).

—. _____   —. _____

_____   _____

—. _____   —. _____

_____   _____

—. _____   —. _____

_____   _____

SEPARATION ANXIETY

BEHAVIORAL DEFINITIONS

1. Exhibits behaviors such as crying, tantruming, or refusing to leave upon separation or anticipated separation from a parent.
2. Demonstrates frequent and severe emotional distress (e.g., tantruming, crying) upon leaving home or with the anticipation of leaving home.
3. Exhibits repeated distress behaviors (e.g., tantruming, crying) when kept away from a parent.
4. Experiences frequent somatic complaints (e.g., headaches, stomachaches, nausea) when separation from home or the attachment figure is anticipated or has occurred.
5. Complains of sleep disturbance when away from home and/or when away from the immediate presence of a parent.
6. Verbalizes persistent and unrealistic worry about possible harm occurring to close attachment figures or excessive fear that they will leave and not return.
7. Avoids being alone by exhibiting clinging and shadowing behaviors toward parent.

—. _____
   _____
—. _____
   _____
—. _____
   _____

LONG-TERM GOALS

1. Separate from the parent without the display of overt distress behaviors.
2. Leave home and enter the classroom or childcare center without overt distress behaviors.

3. Eliminate the somatic complaints accompanying separation.
4. Improve sleep patterns to include the ability to sleep in his/her own room and to sleep through the night.
5. All significant caregivers (e.g., family, school, daycare staff) understand separation anxiety and the need for consistency with the child across settings.

—. _____
   _____
—. _____
   _____
—. _____
   _____

SHORT-TERM OBJECTIVES	**THERAPEUTIC INTERVENTIONS**
1. Parents meet with school staff to discuss concerns regarding separation issues of the child. (1, 2)	1. Arrange for a collaborative conference between the parents and the classroom staff to discuss the separation concerns exhibited by the child at school and home.
	2. Refer the parents to their pediatrician or family physician for a medical evaluation of the child; process the results as they apply to the child's behavior.
2. Cooperate with the evaluation procedures. (3, 4, 5)	3. Establish a series of observations at school and potentially other settings, as suggested by the parents, to form the basis for a behavioral assessment of the child's separation patterns and issues (e.g., stimulus events, behavioral acting out, consequences).
	4. Determine with the parents components of additional evaluation measures, such as behavioral interviews with significant adults

and completion of child behavior rating scales (e.g., Child Behavior Checklist for ages 1½–5 and/or Caregiver-Teacher Report Form for ages 1½–5 by Achenbach).

5. Provide feedback regarding all evaluation outcomes to the family.

3. Reduce the frequency and severity of distress behaviors upon separation. (6, 7, 8)

6. Create a positive behavior support plan with a collaborative team to include the parents, using observational and evaluation information; emphasize elimination of overt behaviors upon separation, and establish a set of reinforcements for self-management upon separation.

7. Match the positive behavior support interventions with goals and values of the family.

8. Teach the child new routines upon separation from the parent (e.g., promptly hanging up his/her coat, promptly putting belongings in his/her locker area, moving directly into a play activity with peers) to replace the maladaptive behaviors; use modeling to teach examples of positive behavior.

4. Establish consistent positive interaction with significant adults in school setting. (9, 10)

9. Work to develop a positive, nurturing, trusting relationship with the child, to provide him/her with a secure environment in which to arrive each day.

10. Give positive reinforcement to any actions by the child that denote trust, affection, or positive feelings toward significant adults in the school setting (e.g., acceptance of being held by a staff member,

5. Exhibit self-confidence in displaying strengths and interests. (11)

6. Readily transition from parent into arrival activities. (12, 13)

7. Parent positively engages in arrival routine. (14, 15, 16)

talking to the staff, playing with the staff, following directions from staff).

11. In an effort to create incentives for the positive behavior support plan and establish a trusting relationship with the child, place an emphasis on the child's interests and talents by developing with the child and family a reinforcement menu based on answering questions such as: What are the child's talents? What does the child like to do? Which peers and teachers make him/her most comfortable? What are his/her favorite toys?

12. Establish a consistent arrival routine with a regular pattern for both the child and the parent.

13. Use welcoming techniques for arrival to include speaking to the child at eye level, escorting the child to his/her place for belongings (which needs to be clearly marked with the child's name), and transition the child to a specific favored play activity in the free-play area.

14. Establish with the parent a communication routine to include asking about routine issues, such as sleep, feeding, basic need concerns; ask specific questions, such as: How is Jon doing this morning? What kind of night did he have? Have there been any concerns? (see *Strategies for Including Children with Special Needs in Early Childhood Settings* by Klein, Cook, and Richardson-Gibbs).

15. When the parent is ready to leave, provide verbal prompts to the child (e.g., "Mommy is leaving now. She will be back in the afternoon after snack time. Give mommy a hug. Tell Mommy goodbye"; see *Strategies for Including Children with Special Needs in Early Childhood Settings* by Klein, Cook, and Richardson-Gibbs).

16. Stay with a carefully planned departure routine with the parent that emphasizes consistency and an exit by the significant adult despite any demonstration of emotional distress by the child.

8. Readily transition from the classroom into a departure routine with parent. (17, 18)

17. When the child is scheduled to depart for the day, follow a routine procedure, such as: (1) give the child a verbal prompt that his/her parent will be arriving soon; (2) assist the child with organizing items for departure; (3) upon the parent's arrival, prompt the child to seek his/her belongings; (4) encourage the child to say goodbye to favored peers and/or the classroom pet; (5) make a specific statement to the child regarding the next day (e.g., "Tomorrow is Friday. We will be making applesauce and celebrating Andrea's birthday. I will see you then"; see *Strategies for Including Children with Special Needs in Early Childhood Settings* by Klein, Cook, and Richardson-Gibbs).

18. Encourage the parent to make the child's departure from school as positive and routine as possible,

9. Show positive attachment to a peer or peers to replace negative behaviors of separation issues. (19, 20)

10. Implement relaxation techniques to decrease the stress of separation and anxiety. (21, 22, 23, 24)

setting a proactive climate for the child's return to the classroom the next time.

19. Promptly upon his/her arrival, pair the child with a favored peer or peers in a favored activity as a motivator for positive integration into the classroom.

20. Use favored peers throughout the day to reinforce and motivate the child to master more anxiety-provoking situations and to be fully involved in classroom activities.

21. Teach the child relaxation techniques by giving specific directions of tensing muscles and then relaxing them, which should be modeled by an adult and pursued several times per week (e.g., push your shoulders up to your ears and pull your head back down into your shoulders; see *Clinical Behavior Therapy with Children* by Ollendic and Cerny).

22. Have the child participate in relaxing experiences at intermittent times during the day (e.g., listening to stories, game-playing with a favored adult and/or peers, eating favorite foods).

23. Teach the child deep breathing exercises as a relaxation technique and as an alternative response to emotional distress.

24. Instruct the child in the turtle technique: When the cue word *turtle* is used, the child is to act like a turtle by physically closing his/her eyes and pulling

arms and legs close to the body, similar to a turtle going into its shell; the child then uses a muscle tensing, muscle relaxation process releasing all tension from his/her body (see "The Turtle Technique: A Method for the Self-Control of Impulsive Behavior" by Schneider and Robin in *Counseling Methods* [Krumboltz and Thoreson, eds.]).

11. Parents set limits and end tolerance for tantruming and clinging behaviors. (25, 26, 27, 28)

25. Provide instruction and support to parents in setting consistent, firm limits when the child engages in overt, negative behaviors (e.g., screaming, refusing to leave, crying loudly, tantrums).

26. Closely communicate with the parents to reinforce the child's effective routines being used at both home and school (e.g., share routines and activities so the child is able to make transition into intact self-management; Does it involve nap time and bed time? Snack time and meal time?); examine with the parents the positive aspects of these routines and how the specifics of a positive routine can be applied to difficult episodes.

27. Explore the parents' interactions with their son/daughter, including their overprotection patterns and their reaction to their child's irrational fears and dependency behaviors; redirect any inconsistencies or reinforcing consequences.

28. Refer the family to counseling services as appropriate.

12. Parents seek resolution to child's nighttime dysfunctional patterns. (29, 30)

29. Advise parents as to a bedtime routine that could include developing a reassuring pattern (e.g., toy to sleep with, story with a parent, parent leaving the child's room in the same manner each evening, leaving a night light on, refusing to remove the child from his/her bed, staying calm but firm in setting limits and giving reassurance).

30. Assist the parent with establishing a plan that reinforces the child for remaining in his/her own room and not showing emotional distress at bedtime or during the night.

13. Parents pursue medical intervention. (31)

31. Should the child's physical symptoms (e.g., headaches, stomachaches) continue after other interventions to reduce separation anxiety have successfully been employed, encourage the parents to seek medical and psychological attention for their child for the somatic issues.

14. Parents express satisfaction with their child's progress and care and work collaboratively with the daycare staff. (32, 33)

32. Create trust with the parents by providing education and training to classroom staff regarding separation anxiety, its treatment, the specific treatment plan for this child, and effective ways to communicate concerns and successes to the parents.

33. Develop with the parents a set of scheduled dates to hold communication meetings with specific agenda items where the child's progress and concerns of home and school can collaboratively be discussed and problem-solved.

SHYNESS/SOCIAL PHOBIA

BEHAVIORAL DEFINITIONS

1. Engages in less than age-appropriate social relationships (e.g., demonstrating very limited or no interactive play skills).
2. Chooses to isolate self by exhibiting hiding behaviors, shrinking away from others, and limited or no eye contact.
3. Exhibits overt, intense emotional distress (e.g., crying, tantrums, unwillingness to move, or clinging to a familiar person) when involved in a feared social setting, event, or performance.
4. Exhibits physiological distress in social setting as exhibited by increased heart rate, muscular tension, trembling, sweating, nausea, and/or diarrhea.
5. Is markedly reluctant to engage in new activities, new settings, or to initiate interaction with involved adults or peers.
6. Demonstrates much greater sensitivity to disapproval, criticism, or rejection by adults or peers than is age-appropriate, frequently resulting in withdrawal or tearfulness.

—. _____
_____
—. _____
_____
—. _____
_____

LONG-TERM GOALS

1. Increase the frequency and duration of age-appropriate social interaction, including interactive play behaviors.

2. Master essential social skills that will enhance peer and adult interactions and relationships.
3. Terminate self-isolating behaviors and significantly increase eye contact.
4. Replace fearful, intense emotional responses (e.g., crying, tantruming) with positive reactions to routine or new social settings, social performances, or transitions.
5. Learn strategies that significantly decrease or eliminate negative physiological responses to anxiety related to social interaction and social performance.
6. Increase positive initiation interactions, to readily and comfortably engage in new social activities and initiate interaction with peers and adults.

—. _____
_____
_____

—. _____
_____
_____

—. _____
_____

SHORT-TERM OBJECTIVES

1. Parents or primary caregivers meet with school staff to discuss concerns regarding the child's social withdrawal behaviors. (1, 2)

2. Participate in evaluation procedures. (3, 4, 5, 6)

THERAPEUTIC INTERVENTIONS

1. Arrange for a collaborative conference between the parents and/or primary caregivers with classroom staff to discuss the child's shyness and self-isolating behavior.

2. Refer the parents and/or primary caregivers to their pediatrician or family physician for a medical evaluation of the child; process the results as they may apply to the child's behavior.

3. Establish a series of observations to form the basis for a behavioral assessment of the child's social interaction patterns.

4. Determine with the parents and/or primary caregiver components of additional evaluation

measures, most likely including play therapy techniques.

5. Assess the child's social interaction patterns, using play therapy techniques and role-playing methods.

6. Provide feedback regarding all evaluation outcomes to the family.

3. Increase social interaction time in response to reinforcement and desensitization strategies. (7, 8, 9, 10)

7. Create a positive behavior support plan with the parents or primary caregivers, using observational and evaluation information and targeting the social withdrawal behaviors in the group setting with positive reinforcement for socially integrative actions by the child.

8. Employ a step-by-step sequential distraction/desensitization process with the child in a small peer group setting by employing the following: (1) place some of the child's favorite toys near peers; (2) show the child the toys; (3) have peers engage in parallel play next to the child with some of his/her favored toys; (4) establish a series of these parallel play scenarios, with an increase in time the child spends next to peers without emotional distress.

9. Couple the increased time the child spends in parallel play with a favored experience (e.g., play the child's favorite music while he/she is engaged in play next to peers).

10. Reinforce the child with additional positive incentives for any interactive play behavior.

4. Implement relaxation techniques to decrease the stress of shyness and social contact. (11, 12, 13)

11. Teach the child relaxation techniques by giving specific directions of muscle movement, which should be modeled by an adult and pursued several times per week (e.g., "push your shoulders up to your ears and pull your head back down into your shoulders"; see *Clinical Behavior Therapy with Children* by Ollendic and Cerny).

12. While next to play-engaged peers, have the child participate in relaxing experiences (e.g., listening to stories, game-playing with a favored adult with peers joining in, eating favorite foods).

13. Teach the child deep breathing exercises as a relaxation technique and as an alternative response to emotional distress.

5. Increase the frequency and quality of social initiations with peers in response to modeling and reinforcement procedures. (14, 15)

14. Use modeling techniques to teach the child how to greet a peer and how to offer a toy as a way to begin play; reinforce the child with frequent physical and verbal reinforcers when the child is able to move next to a peer, give a greeting, and offer a toy to the peer.

15. Use a modeling and reinforcement procedure as follows to teach the child appropriate social interactive behaviors: (1) help the child use relaxation techniques to reduce his/her anxiety; (2) have a favored adult model a play activity (e.g., playing a game, sharing a book, using play dough) with a peer while the child watches, reinforcing the child for watching

the activity; (3) direct the favored adult to move with the child into the activity and to continue to model appropriate peer play and interactive behavior; (4) reinforce the child at short intervals for remaining in the activity with peers; (5) finally, direct the adult to withdraw from the activity while continuing to reinforce the child for his/her ongoing participation.

6. Demonstrate greater competence with specific social skills. (16)

16. Use modeling, puppetry, and individualized and small group instruction to teach basic social skills to the child (e.g., smiling, eye contact, greetings, simple conversation) to boost his/her confidence in relating to others.

7. Demonstrate increased quality and frequency of social interaction across settings outside of school. (17, 18, 19)

17. Make a visit to the child's home to explore his/her social needs and skills in this environment.

18. Train the parents and/or primary caregivers in basic shaping techniques of positive reinforcement and modeling, so they may assist the child at home and in other social experiences (e.g., church, neighborhood play group); stress the importance of the family modeling positive social commitments and interactions themselves without anxiety.

19. Obtain parental feedback as to the child's success and needs in social settings; encourage the parents to guide the child into engagement in select social events, which match the child's strengths and interests.

8. Parents or primary caregivers identify how they may be contributing to the child's social anxiety or shyness. (20, 21, 22, 23)

20. Discuss in a sensitive manner with the family and/or primary caregiver how their interactions with the child could be a factor in the social phobic behavior of their child; emphasize that overprotection of the child because he/she is shy is counterproductive.

21. Process with the family and/or primary caregiver ways in which routine, advance preparation for transitions, and unconditional reassurance can assist in reducing the child's anxiety.

22. Establish with the family and/or primary caregivers a schedule of transition events, which positively prepare the child for participation in peer activities and experiences so as to decrease anxiety.

23. Evaluate the parents' pattern of social interaction to assess whether they are modeling fear and anxiety related to interacting with others; refer them for treatment or to a social skills training group, if indicated.

9. Parents or primary caregivers verbalize realistic expectations for the child. (24, 25)

24. Assist the family and/or primary caregiver in deepening their understanding of the child's developmental age so they can establish reasonable expectations for the child, given his/her age and fears.

25. Refer the family to a specialist working with young children and shyness/social phobia issues should the severity and duration of withdrawal behaviors remain extreme, and there is little or no progress toward resolution.

10. Parents or primary caregivers work as full partners with classroom staff in maintaining a quality program and experience for their child and express satisfaction with child's progress. (26, 27)

26. Establish and maintain frequent, open communication with the parents regarding issues, concerns, and successes of their child.

27. Select a staff member to serve as a primary contact to any other agencies or services providing support to the child, to coordinate all efforts in best meeting the child's social needs and those of his/her family.

—. _____
   _____

—. _____
   _____

—. _____
   _____

—. _____
   _____

—. _____
   _____

—. _____
   _____

SLEEP ISSUES

BEHAVIORAL DEFINITIONS

1. Exhibits difficulty falling asleep or remaining asleep.
2. Shows emotional distress (e.g., crying, waking parents, wanting to sleep with parents) while failing to fall or remain asleep.
3. Awakens in considerable distress due to recurring frightening dreams.
4. Refuses to sleep in own bed, making demands on parents to be close by.
5. Exhibits prolonged sleep and/or excessive daytime napping without feeling rested, but is continually tired.

___. _____
_____

___. _____
_____

___. _____
_____

LONG-TERM GOALS

1. Fall asleep calmly and remain asleep without presence of parents.
2. Appear to be well rested and energized during waking hours.
3. Virtually eliminate the occurrence of fearful, anxiety-produced dreams.
4. Terminate excessive, prolonged sleep patterns.
5. Sleep in own room, separate from parents and through the night.

___. _____
_____

___. _____
_____

SHORT-TERM OBJECTIVES

1. Parents meet with classroom staff to explain their concerns regarding the child's sleep dysfunction. (1, 2)

2. Parents pursue a medical exam for their child to rule out physical concerns. (3, 4, 5)

3. Parents seek hypotheses within the family as to the potential origins of the child's sleep dysfunction. (6, 7, 8, 9)

THERAPEUTIC INTERVENTIONS

1. Meet with parents to listen to their concerns regarding the child's sleep dysfunction.

2. Share with the family how the child responds to naptime and how excessive sleep or sleep deprivation impacts his/her behavior in the classroom setting.

3. Refer the parents to the child's physician for a medical evaluation; ask the parents to share with staff any salient physical issues (e.g., seizure disorder, ear, nose, or throat issues) identified during the medical exam.

4. Facilitate the staff to implement special provisions or accommodations as identified by medical personnel in terms of the child's medical needs in the classroom setting.

5. Refer the family to a psychologist, child psychiatrist, or physician specializing in sleep issues and sleep assessment of young children.

6. Ask a designated staff member or special education professional (e.g., school psychologist, school social worker) to explore issues with the family that potentially cause the sleep problems for the child (e.g., trauma, stress in the family, marital strife, parental substance abuse, sibling conflict).

7. The designated staff member, with written permission from the parents, communicates with the professional treating or evaluating the child (e.g., child psychologist, child psychiatrist) regarding potential reasons for the child's sleep dysfunction, if it indeed originates within the family.

8. Facilitate assimilation of recommendations from the outside clinician into the classroom setting, making accommodations as appropriate.

9. Make a referral to the local child protection service agency, as required by law, of any significant trauma involving physical abuse, sexual abuse, and/or neglect of the child, if suspected as a reason for the child's sleep dysfunction.

4. The family identifies and accepts sources of conflict or stressors impacting the child and his/her sleep issues. (10, 11)

10. Encourage the family's involvement with an outside clinician who can assist them in resolving family issues that contribute to the child's sleep disturbance.

11. Implement recommendations from the family and professional working with the family in an attempt to assist the child socially/emotionally and provide continuity between home and classroom setting.

5. Parents set limits to reduce manipulative behaviors of child. (12, 13)

12. Encourage the family to consult with the outside clinician in setting firm limits on the child's manipulative behaviors.

13. Classroom staff follow the limit-setting techniques used at home.

6. Follow a specific bedtime routine at home. (14)

14. Parents collaborate with the outside clinician to create an

effective bedtime routine (e.g., taking a bath, having a story read, listening to quiet music), thereby reducing problematic sleep-related behaviors; caregivers closely adhere to this specific routine.

7. Follow a specific naptime routine in the classroom/daycare setting. (15)

15. Direct the classroom staff to implement a somewhat similar routine for naptime as is used at home and adhere to the specific routine, to keep continuity and structure for the child.

8. Implement relaxation techniques to induce calming and the initiation of sleep. (16)

16. Both parents at home and classroom staff teach the child a progressive relaxation script to help induce sleep (e.g., deep breathing techniques, progressive muscle relaxation of feet, legs, thighs, stomach, hands, arms/chest, shoulders, face followed by a repeat of deep breathing techniques; see *Emotional and Behavioral Problems of Young Children* by Gimpel and Holland).

9. Adults implement a gradual extinction model to terminate the child's crying during the night or at naptime. (17, 18, 19)

17. Teach the parents and classroom staff to use a gradual extinction treatment plan, where the adult is permitted to briefly check on the child (e.g., for 15 seconds) but must wait before entering the room (e.g., 10 seconds) once crying has started (see *Infant and Toddler Mental Health* by Maldonado-Duran [ed.]).

18. Progressively increase the adult waiting time by 5 minutes after each checking to teach the child that more crying decreases adult contact.

19. Urge the parents and classroom staff to systematically not respond to the child's cries during the night or naptime after being assured the child is safe.

10. Parents and classroom staff implement the cosleeping intervention model to terminate the child's crying during the night or at naptime. (20, 21)

20. Direct the primary caregiver to sleep in the child's bedroom for 1 week without other involvement with the child during the night; the concept is to reassure the child that the adult will not disappear during the night (see *Infant and Toddler Mental Health* by Maldonado-Duran [ed.]).

21. Facilitate the implementation of a modified version of the cosleeping intervention model in the classroom setting, where an adult remains close when the child is taking a nap but does not respond to crying with the exception of being present as appropriate.

11. Adults implement the concept of a bedtime pass to extinguish the child's crying and not staying in bed. (22, 23)

22. Teach the parents to issue a bedtime pass prior to sleep for the child who wakes in the night and leaves the bedroom; the child must use the pass for a one-time out-of-the-bedroom reason (e.g., using the bathroom, getting a drink), but all crying is ignored and the child must return promptly to the bedroom (see "The Bedtime Pass" by Friman, Hoff, Schnoes, Freeman, Woods, and Blum in *Archives of Pediatrics and Adolescent Medicine*).

23. Direct the classroom staff to adapt the "bedtime pass" concept to naptime in the classroom setting.

12. Parents express progressive success with the child's sleeping issues and verbalize satisfaction with staff and their support. (24, 25)

24. Establish an ongoing, preferred form of communication with the family (e.g., e-mail, weekly phone contact, communication notebook) to exchange information on a regular basis regarding concerns, patterns, and successful days and nights.

25. Establish an intermittent conference schedule with the parents to maintain an open exchange of information; to make contact with outside professionals (e.g., psychologist, physician) as appropriate to facilitate the child's progress and needs.

__. _____
_____
__. _____
_____
__. _____
_____

__. _____
_____
__. _____
_____
__. _____
_____

SOCIAL SKILLS DELAY

BEHAVIORAL DEFINITIONS

1. Poor peer and adult verbal and nonverbal communication skills, including a lack of reciprocity, even in simple conversation.
2. Responds to conflict or correction with opposition and/or angry tantrums.
3. Has a history of being destructive to own property or the property of others, out of anger or simple disregard.
4. A delay in being able to use cooperation skills, including sharing toys and materials with peers, helping others, and demonstrating compliance with rules.
5. An inability to ask for assistance or information.
6. A consistent yielding to negative peer pressure (e.g., following the negative behavior of peers rather than making positive behavior choices).
7. A lack of empathy and concern for the feelings of others.

—. _____
   _____
   _____
—. _____
   _____
   _____
—. _____
   _____

LONG-TERM GOALS

1. Improve verbal and nonverbal communication skills with adults and peers, showing success with conversation.
2. Demonstrate the ability to interact cooperatively and kindly with peers.
3. Demonstrate increased self-management skills, using words or compliance in stressful settings, in place of aggressive acts toward peers and adults.

4. Exhibit responsible behavior in relation to compliance with rules, taking care of own property, and showing respect for the property of others.

—. _____

_____

—. _____

_____

—. _____

_____

SHORT-TERM OBJECTIVES

1. Parents identify concerns regarding the child's social interaction skills and provide relevant family background information. (1, 2)

2. Engage in routine activities across multiple settings while being observed and assessed. (3)

THERAPEUTIC INTERVENTIONS

1. Interview the parents to ascertain their concerns about their child's social skills, obtain relevant background information and develop a plan for how the social skills assessment will be completed.

2. Ask the parent to complete a social skills rating scale (e.g., *The Social Skills Rating System* by Gresham and Elliott) and a problem behavior scale (e.g., *Preschool and Kindergarten Behavior Scales* by Merrell) as part of the child's social skills assessment.

3. Complete a functional assessment of behavior involving direct systematic observations of the child across multiple settings, examining antecedents and sequential and consequent conditions related to specific behaviors (see "Functional Behavioral Assessments and Intervention Plans in Early Intervention Settings" by LaRoque, Brown, and Johnson in *Infants and Young Children*).

3. Participate in behavioral role-plays with school professional as part of the assessment. (4)

4. Have the child engage in specific role-play activities centered around identified behavioral and social concerns (e.g., respectfully obtaining a desired toy from another child or obediently following directions at snack time); assess his/her social and problem-solving skills.

4. Teacher identifies concerns regarding the child's social skill deficits. (5, 6)

5. Interview the preschool teacher regarding the child's social interaction patterns in the classroom setting; have behavior rating scales completed by appropriate preschool staff.

6. Develop a list of the child's strengths and needs that must be considered when developing a treatment plan.

5. Parents and teachers collaborate with the school mental health professional in developing an interaction plan. (7)

7. Organize the observational data from the functional assessment of behavior, the data from parents, teacher(s), and role-playing activities, to create a positive behavior support plan that targets the child's social skills across multiple settings and that takes into account his/her strengths and needs (see *Positive Behavior Support for ALL Michigan Students: Creating Environments That Assure Learning* [Michigan Department of Education—Office of Special Education and Early Intervention Services]); share this plan with teacher and parents for their reaction and support.

6. Learn and implement positive social initiation strategies. (8, 9, 10)

8. Engage the child in entry dialogue to assist him/her with learning how to enter a play group, (e.g., "Let's listen to what they're doing here. What are they playing? What could you do to help with that?";

see "Social Acceptance: Strategies
Children Use and How Teachers
Can Help Children Learn Them"
by Hazen, Black, and Fleming-
Johnson in *Young Children,*
1984, September, pp. 26–36).

9. Using questioning and acting as
   an interpreter, have the teacher
   (or other school professional),
   redirect and guide the child
   with verbal and nonverbal cues
   through nonadaptive initiation to
   play (e.g., when the child grabs a
   toy from another, the adult says,
   "Listen to what Tommy is saying.
   Why doesn't he want to give you
   the toy now? Can you think of
   something else you and Tommy
   could do together?").

10. Direct a socially adept peer to
    initiate and maintain social inter-
    action with the child; point out
    the adept peer's positive skills for
    him/her to emulate.

7. Increase the frequency of
   targeted prosocial behaviors.
   (11, 12, 13, 14, 15)

11. Give the child an opportunity
    to practice social skills with one
    other child by arranging a special
    activity that can lead to coopera-
    tive interaction (e.g., move the
    two children to a water table or
    sandbox with toys to share, pro-
    vide them with a box of dress-up
    clothes to share, let them work
    together picking up a specific play
    area).

12. Bring the child into a carefully
    orchestrated small play group
    supervised by an adult in a private
    area in the classroom, where there
    is less confusion, to allow him/her
    to practice prosocial behavior
    (e.g., puppet theater, playhouse,
    loft area, book corner).

13. Organize a cooperative learning activity to allow the child to participate in a setting that requires him/her to "cooperate, share, and assist" others to complete a task (e.g., create special food with others for snack time, make a mural with others for classroom display, use puppets to act out a favorite story; see "Best Practices in Preschool Social Skills Training" by Elliot, McKevitt, and DiPerna in *Best Practices in School Psychology IV*).

14. Provide the child with modeling of prosocial behaviors (both verbal and nonverbal) by a peer, by a supervising adult, by puppetry, and through exposure to videotaped scenes of appropriate behavior (see "A Social Skills Program for Developmentally Delayed Preschoolers" by Matson, Fee, Coe, and Smith in *Child and Family Behavior Therapy,* 1991, pp. 227–242).

15. Help the child transfer instructional prompts into desired, socially appropriate behaviors using coaching procedures (e.g., the child is given the rules for a specific desired behavior; then the selected social skill is rehearsed with the coach; finally, as the child implements the behavior, the coach gives specific feedback and suggestions for future behavior; see "Best Practices in Preschool Social Skills Training" by Elliott, McKevitt, and DiPernain in *Best Practices in School Psychology IV*).

8. Demonstrate a decrease in undesirable behaviors that compete with prosocial actions. (16)

9. Implement social skills learned from social interventions used with all children in the classroom. (17)

10. Demonstrate social sensitivity and empathic awareness toward peers and adults. (18, 19, 20)

16. Develop a schedule whereby the child receives reinforcement for any socially appropriate behavior, increasing the frequency of these behaviors while extinguishing competing undesirable behaviors.

17. Utilize the Responsive Classroom approach to build social skills of all children in the class; integrate acceptance, positive interpersonal relationships and responsibility into daily instruction including six major elements: (1) morning meeting; (2) classroom organization; (3) rules and logical consequences; (4) guided discovery; (5) academic choice time; and (6) assessment and reporting (see *The Responsive Classroom Approach to Instruction* by Charney and Wood).

18. Use teachable moments (e.g., when another child is sad or ill) to model an empathetic response for the child; ask him/her to rehearse an adaptive empathic response after it is modeled.

19. Read salient children's literature on the topic of empathy (e.g., *Two Good Friends* by Delton) to assist the child in learning cooperation and sensitivity to others; point out how empathy is demonstrated in the story.

20. Engage the child in a simple role-playing activity with one or two other children, where both positive and negative feelings are acted out and emphasis by the adult is on showing care and concern for others when sadness or frustration are displayed.

11. Parents collaborate with school personnel on targeting intervention techniques on specific social behaviors of their child in the home. (21, 22)

12. Parents focus on helping their child generalize social skills to home and the community. (23, 24)

13. Report a sense of enjoyment with and pride in school activities. (25, 26, 27)

21. Teach the parents techniques to use at home to increase the child's prosocial behavior and decrease or extinguish undesirable interfering behavior; keep the techniques and target behaviors consistent with the school goals and interventions.

22. Assist the parents with learning to effectively play with their child at home, encouraging them to model socially appropriate concepts of play to include initiation of play, sharing, cooperation, helping others, and exhibiting empathy.

23. Encourage the parents to consistently apply reinforcement techniques used at school, across settings in the community (e.g., stores, church, daycare) to promote generalization of the child's prosocial behaviors; help parents make adjustments and adaptations of desired techniques; if necessary.

24. Offer parent training or refer parents to resources in the community for parent training (e.g., *1-2-3 Magic: Training Your Preschoolers and Preteens to Do What You Want* by Phelan, *Defiant Children: A Clinician's Manual for Parent Training—2nd ed.* by Barkley, or *Parenting with Love and Logic* by Cline and Fay).

25. Engage the child in confidence-building tasks that focus on being socially responsible (e.g., feeding the classroom fish, delivering attendance information to the office, completing a special errand for the teacher).

26. Create opportunities for the child to have choices involving tasks and materials of high interest that spur motivation (e.g., completing puzzles, playing favorite games, using gross motor toys and equipment on the playground, creating an art project to take home, bringing a special toy or book from home to share with the group).

27. Conduct Affirmation Interviews where the child is interviewed in front of a large group and given special attention by being asked simple, nonthreatening and interesting questions that are individualized to him/her (e.g., What is your favorite sandwich? What place would you like to visit? What is something you enjoy doing?; see *The Friendly Classroom for a Small Planet: Handbook of the Children's Creative Response to Conflict Program* by Prutzman, Burger, Bodenhamer, and Stern).

14. Participate in individual play therapy sessions to work through any significant emotional or behavioral issues interfering with prosocial development. (28)

15. Parents work as full partners with school staff in maintaining quality interventions and programming for their child and express satisfaction with his/her progress. (29, 30)

28. Involve the child in short-term counseling with a school mental health professional, placing emphasis on critical issues for him/her that influence his/her social behavior.

29. Establish and maintain frequent, open communication with the parents regarding issues and successes of their child; select a method of communication most acceptable to the parent (e.g., home/school communication notebooks, weekly phone call, e-mail).

30. Refer the parents to a local support group and/or a national organization to facilitate their information gathering in relation to a young child's social skill development.

—. _____   —. _____
   _____   _____

—. _____   —. _____
   _____   _____

—. _____   —. _____
   _____   _____

VISION DEFICITS/BLINDNESS

BEHAVIORAL DEFINITIONS

1. Experiences a vision loss or deficit that adversely impacts overall development and/or functioning across environments.
2. Has been identified as legally visually impaired or blind as a result of a comprehensive evaluation by a pediatric ophthalmologist or optometrist.
3. Vision loss or deficit originates from trauma before, during, or after birth, infection, or retinopathy due to prematurity.
4. Vision loss or impairment originates from a congenital eye condition (e.g., albinism, amblyopia, cataracts, glaucoma, strabismus, optic nerve atrophy).
5. Specialized techniques, equipment, and materials are required to assist the child with progress in the domains of cognition, communication, motor, self-help, sensory, and social skills.

—. _____
_____
—. _____
_____
—. _____
_____

LONG-TERM GOALS

1. Respond to sensory modality experiences and training in acquiring salient knowledge of his/her environment at an appropriate developmental level.
2. Develop listening and tactile skills commensurate with learning potential across various settings (e.g., home, school, community).
3. Learn orientation and mobility skills sufficient to begin developing inde-

pendence skills across various environments (e.g., home, school, community).

4. Demonstrate increasing levels of competence and feelings of greater self-esteem.

5. Achieve goals and objectives identified in the Individualized Educational Team Plan emphasizing competencies across various domains (i.e., functional skills, social skills, pre-academics, and language).

6. Parents process acceptance of their child's visual deficits, establishing realistic expectations and seeking assistance and resources to meet child and family needs.

—. _____

_____

—. _____

_____

—. _____

_____

SHORT-TERM OBJECTIVES	THERAPEUTIC INTERVENTIONS
1. Cooperate with a comprehensive visual examination. (1)	1. Refer the family to a pediatric ophthalmologist or optometrist for a comprehensive vision examination for their child.
2. Participate in a multifaceted multidisciplinary evaluation of strengths and weaknesses of vision, language, psychosocial, and intellectual development as appropriate. (2)	2. Organize a multidisciplinary evaluation team to assess the child in areas of functional vision, vision efficiency, low vision aids, intellectual functioning, gross and fine motor skills, language development, listening skills, psychosocial development, orientation and mobility, self-care, and self-help skills; formulate recommendations from assessment data.
3. Parents participate in the Individualized Educational Planning Team process and collaborate on recommendations with school staff. (3)	3. Meet with the parents to share vision, medical, and evaluation information and to create an Individualized Educational Plan.

4. Demonstrate the ability to identify sounds and to accurately associate them with a specific activity. (4, 5, 6, 7, 8)

4. Provide fixed sounds that help the child establish reference points to vital places in various relevant environments, such as placing wind chimes near a window or a ticking clock above a door (see *Children with Visual Impairments: Social Interaction, Language and Learning* by Webster and Roe).

5. Create and implement listening activities that allow the child to practice locating sounds.

6. Organize the classroom into divided, well-designed spaces, each with a specific function for the child to learn.

7. Assist the child with identifying natural sounds in his/her environment (e.g., a telephone, a police or fire siren, a doorbell) for discrimination and association purposes.

8. Introduce functional activities that offer the child opportunities to experience sounds and learning to associate them with useful tasks (e.g., waking up to music from a clock radio; turning off an alarm clock; turning on and off a water faucet and washing his/her hands; turning on, listening to, and turning off a CD player; flushing a toilet after use).

5. Cooperate and work closely with the Orientation and Mobility Specialist to master basic mobility skills across salient environments. (9, 10, 11, 12)

9. Establish priorities of mobility through a collaboration between the Orientation and Mobility Specialist and the family, matching those priorities to developmental skills (e.g., learning routes to the bathroom while working on toileting skills).

10. Have the Orientation and Mobility Specialist analyze salient travel routes within the home and school that the child is likely to follow for safety, and necessary modifications, sharing this information in detail with the family and educational staff.

11. Organize training of the classroom staff, the family, and the Orientation and Mobility Specialist in implementing mobility techniques, skills, and use of equipment individualized for the child.

12. Arrange for a home visit by the Orientation and Mobility Specialist to assist the family with strategies for the child's movement throughout the home and yard, attending to issues of safety, use of space, and accessibility to essential items.

6. Identify various objects through tactile exploration. (13, 14, 15, 16)

13. Teach the child how to effectively explore objects, incorporating how to surface the detail of an object and the needed safety and risk factors involved.

14. Provide opportunities for the child to explore a range of materials (e.g., feathers, a sponge, sand, vegetable oil) that bring about greater tactile awareness and learning.

15. Give chances for the child to experience contact with movement (e.g., blowing, brushing, tickling, stroking) to increase tactile skills and awareness (see *Children with Visual Impairments: Social Interaction, Language and Learning* by Webster and Roe).

7. Demonstrate increased use of developmentally appropriate verbal and nonverbal communication skills. (17, 18, 19, 20)

16. Ensure the child has a selection of toys that offer different textures, sounds, shapes, and functions, which may motivate the child to frequently explore objects with his/her hands (see *Children with Visual Impairments: Social Interaction, Language and Learning* by Webster and Roe).

17. Acknowledge and expand the child's existing communication attempts, responding with imitation and further language to assist him/her with continuing to communicate.

18. Describe persons and objects to the child that are of particular interest to him/her, giving meaningful language input to the child whenever possible by explaining and describing but not overwhelming him/her with information.

19. Set high expectations for the child to verbally communicate his/her wants, needs, wishes, and desires, and expect him/her to complete these verbalizations to his/her greatest potential.

20. Assist the child with acquiring knowledge about nonverbal communication and gestures (e.g., smiling, waving, pointing, nodding) by explaining to the child when and why these cues are used and reinforcing the child for using such gestures as part of communication when developmentally appropriate.

8. Parents coordinate their efforts to build the child's language/communication skills

21. Facilitate the parents working with vision and language specialists and classroom staff on similar

with the classroom staff and the language specialist. (21)

9. Demonstrate pre-academic concepts and abstract reasoning as a precursor to school readiness skills. (22, 23, 24, 25)

language strategies, to provide consistency for the child, allowing for optimum progress.

22. Use frequent hands-on activities (e.g., feeling objects and naming them, exploring objects by touch and being given several word choices of what the object could be, going on a field trip to experience various objects by touch and sounds) to assist the child in learning names of objects and their function.

23. Teach the child categorization skills by playing matching games, finding objects by tactile skills, labeling how objects are alike and different, and associating objects by function (see *Early Focus: Working with Young Blind and Visually Impaired Children and Their Families* by Pogrund, Fazzi, and Lampert).

24. Teach the child problem-solving skills by using guessing games (e.g., feeling objects in a bag and guessing their identity), finding objects by tactile skills, labeling how objects are alike and different, and associating objects by function (see *Early Focus: Working with Young Blind and Visually Impaired Children and Their Families* by Pogrund, Fazzi, and Lampert).

25. Facilitate a collaboration between the teacher of the early childhood visually impaired or the consultant for the visually impaired with classroom staff in incorporating daily learning activities that accentuate concept learning and

abstract reasoning (e.g., touching the mail while visiting the post office, walking with a mail carrier to understand the concept of sending and receiving mail).

10. Demonstrate pre-literacy book skills through listening to books being read and tactile involvement with books. (26, 27, 28)

26. Read to the child frequently in a colorful, expressive manner, describing pictures in the book and interactively discussing content with the child.

27. Offer picture books to the child that have a tactile dimension (e.g., finger holes, different textures, items that pop out) to stimulate interest.

28. Teach preliteracy book skills to include identification of the top and bottom of a page, page turning, and left-to-right sequence.

11. Exhibit competencies with Braille readiness skills. (29, 30, 31)

29. Provide instruction in tactile discrimination skills to include awareness of tactile differences, tolerance of tactile surfaces, recognition of tactile stimuli, and understanding the purpose and use of various tactile stimuli as a precursor to learning Braille (see *Early Focus: Working with Young Blind and Visually Impaired Children and Their Families* by Pogrund, Fazzi, and Lampert).

30. Label in Braille toys, books, and items throughout the classroom to expose the child to the Braille code.

31. Expose the child to published Braille-readiness and reading programs to assist him/her with preparation for future use of Braille as a methodology for reading.

12. Implement appropriate social interaction skills with peers and adults. (32, 33, 34)

32. Provide the child with a variety of physical and verbal contacts with peers and adults across different settings and activities.

33. Strategically organize activities in which the child is the center of an activity and where interaction between the child and peers can be somewhat guided and facilitated as appropriate (e.g., organize a game such as Duck, Duck, Goose, promoting the selection of the visually impaired child by peers, lead the child around the circle helping him/her to select a peer, then reorchestrate the game such that the visually impaired child is first to select others).

34. Instruct adults to give prompts at salient times to facilitate positive interaction between the child and peers (e.g., saying to the child, "Sarah is calling you. If you want to play with her, she is next to the slide.").

13. Parents express satisfaction with their child's adjustment to the classroom and his/her overall progress. (35, 36)

35. Give in-service training to all involved staff prior to the child attending the classroom center, with best practice techniques and methods presented, providing ongoing training as needed, using a child-based, strength-based approach.

36. Establish a routine communication format for exchanging information with the family, discussing accomplishments of the child, concerns, needs, and potential resources to help ensure his/her success.

—. _____

_____

—. _____

_____

—. _____

_____

—. _____

_____

—. _____

_____

—. _____

_____

Appendix A

PARENT SELF-HELP BIBLIOGRAPHY

Aggressive Behavior

Bronson, M. B. (2000). *Self-Regulation in Early Childhood: Nature and Nurture.* New York: Guilford.

Greene, R. W. (2001). *The Explosive Child: A New Approach for Understanding and Parenting Easily Frustrated and Chronically Inflexible Children.* New York: HarperCollins.

Lynn, G. T. (2000). *Survival Strategies for Parenting Children with Bipolar Disorder.* London: Jessica Kingsley.

Articulation/Voice Concerns

Hamaguchi, P. (2001). *Childhood Speech, Language and Listening Problems—What Every Parent Should Know.* New York: Wiley.

Martin, K. L. (1997). *Does My Child Have a Speech Problem?* Chicago: Chicago Review.

Attachment Concerns

Greenspan, S. (1995). *The Challenging Child.* Reading, MA: Perseus Books.

Magid, K., McKelvey, C, A., and Schroeder, P. (1989). *High Risk: Children Without a Conscience.* New York: Bantam.

Turecki, S. (1985). *The Difficult Child.* New York: Bantam.

Attention/Focus

Barkley, R. A. (2000). *Taking Charge of ADHD, Revised Edition: The Complete, Authoritative Guide for Parents.* New York: Guilford.

Hallowell, E. M., and Ratey, J. J. (1995). *Driven to Distraction: Recognizing and Coping with Attention Deficit Disorder from Childhood through Adulthood.* New York: Touchstone.

Lawlis, F., and McGraw, P. (2004). *The ADD Answer: How to Help Your Child Now: With Questionnaires and Family-Centered Action Plans to Meet Your Child's Specific Needs.* New York: Viking.

Reimers, C. L., and Brunger, B. A. (1999). *ADHD in the Young Child: Driven to Re-Direction: A Book for Parents and Teachers.* North Branch, MN: Specialty.

Autism

Hamilton, L. M. (2000). *Facing Autism: Give Parents Reasons for Hope and Guidance for Help.* Colorado Springs, CO: Waterbrook.

Moor, J. (2002). *Playing, Laughing and Learning with Children on the Autism Spectrum: A Practical Resource of Play Ideas for Parents and Caregivers.* London: Jessica Kingsley.

Stacey, P. (2003). *The Boy Who Loved Windows: Opening the Heart and Mind of a Child with Autism.* Cambridge, MA: Da Capo.

Wheeler, M. (1998). *Toilet Training for Individuals with Autism and Related Disorders.* Arlington, TX: Future Horizons.

Depression

Cytryn, L., and McKnew, D. (1998). *Growing Up Sad: Childhood Depression and Its Treatment.* New York: W.W. Norton.

Fitzgerald, H. (1992). *The Grieving Child: A Parent's Guide.* New York: Simon & Schuster.

Eating Concerns

Macht, J. (2002). *Poor Eaters: Helping Children Who Refuse to Eat.* Philadelphia: Perseus.

Satter, E. (1987). *How to Get Your Kid to Eat But Not Too Much.* Palo Alto, CA: Bull.

Wilkoff, W. G. (1998). *Coping with a Picky Eater: A Guide for the Perplexed Parent.* New York: Fireside.

Elimination Concerns

Clarke, J. (2003). *Encopresis.* London: Jessica Kingsley.

Galvin, M. (1991). *Clouds and Clocks: A Story for Children Who Soil.* Washington, DC: Magination.

Mack, A. (1990). *Dry All Night: The Picture Book Technique That Stops Bedwetting.* New York: Little, Brown.

Maizels, M., Rosenbaum, D., and Keating, B. (1999). *Getting to Dry: How to Help Your Child Overcome Bedwetting.* Boston: Harvard Common.

Mills, J. C., Crowley, R. J., and Cook, G. (1989). *Sammy the Elephant and Mr. Camel: A Story to Help Children Overcome Enuresis While Discovering Self-Appreciation.* Washington, DC: Magination.

Expressive Language Delay

Agin, M. C., Geng, L. F., and Nicholl, M. (2003). *The Late Talker: What To Do If Your Child Isn't Talking Yet.* New York: St. Martin's.

Apel, K., and Masterson, J. (2001). *Beyond Baby Talk: From Sounds to Sentences, A Parent's Complete Guide to Language Development.* Roseville, CA: Prima.

Baron, N. (1992). *Growing Up with Language: How Children Learn to Talk.* Philadelphia: Perseus.

Hamaguchi, P. A. (2001). *Childhood Speech, Language and Listening Problems.* New York: Wiley.

Sowell, T. (2001). *The Einstein Syndrome.* New York: Basic Books.

Generalized Anxiety

Dacey, J. S., and Fiore, L. B. (2001). *Your Anxious Child: How Parents and Teachers Can Relieve Anxiety in Children.* Hoboken, NJ: Wiley.

Foxman, P. (2004). *The Worried Child: Recognizing Anxiety in Children and Helping Them Heal.* Alameda, CA: Hunter House.

Goldstein, S., Brooks, R. B., and Hagar, K. (2003). *Seven Steps to Help Your Child Worry Less: A Family Guide.* North Branch, MN: Specialty.

Lite, L., and Hartigan, M. (1996). *Boy and a Bear: The Children's Relaxation Book.* North Branch, MN: Specialty.

Rapee, R., Spence, S., Cobham, V., and Wigxall, A. (2000). *Helping Your Anxious Child.* Oakland, CA: New Harbinger.

Wagner, A. P. (2002). *Worried No More: Help and Hope for Anxious Children.* New York: Lighthouse.

Hearing Deficits/Deafness

Candlish, P. A. M. (1996). *Not Deaf Enough: Raising a Child Who is Hard of Hearing.* Washington, DC: Alexander Graham Bell Association for the Deaf and Hard of Hearing.
Mapp, I. (2004). *Essential Readings on Stress and Coping among Parents of Deaf and Hearing-Impaired Children.* New York: Gordian Knot Books.
Medwid, D. J., and Weston, D. C. (1995). *Kid Friendly Parenting with Deaf and Hard of Hearing Children: A Treasury of Fun Activities toward Better Behavior.* Washington, DC: Gallaudet University Press.
Schuyler, V., and Sowers, J. (1998). *For Families: A Guidebook for Helping Your Young Deaf or Hard of Hearing Child Learn to Listen and Communicate.* Portland, OR: Hearing & Speech Institute.
Stewart, D. A., and Clarke, B. R. (2003). *Literacy and Your Deaf Child: What Every Parent Should Know.* Washington, DC: Gallaudet University Press.

Medically Fragile

Freeman, J. M., Vining, E., and Pillas, D. J. (1997). *Seizures and Epilepsy in Childhood: A Guide for Parents.* Baltimore: The Johns Hopkins University Press.
Hochstadt, N. J. (1991). *The Medically Complex Child: The Transition to Home Care.* Chur, Switzerland: Harwood Academic.
Loving, G. (1993). *Parenting a Child with Diabetes.* Lincolnwood, IL: Lowell House.

Mild Cognitive Delays

Newman, S., and Mellersh, J. (1999). *Small Steps Forward: Using Games and Activities to Help Your Pre-School Child with Special Needs.* London: Jessica Kingsley.
Pueschel, S. M. (1995). *A Parent's Guide to Down Syndrome.* Baltimore: Paul H. Brookes.
Smith, R. E., and Shriver, E. Kennedy. (1993). *Children with Mental Retardation: A Parent's Guide.* Bethesda, MD: Woodbine House.

Moderate/Severe Cognitive Impairment

Barber, B. L., Brightman, A. J., Blachen, J. B., and Heifetz, L. J. (2003). *Steps to Independence: Teaching Everyday Skills to Children with Special Needs.* Baltimore: Paul H. Brookes.
Greenspan, S. I., Weider, S., and Simon, R. (1998). *The Child with Special Needs: Encouraging Intellectual and Emotional Growth.* Boston: Addison-Wesley.
Pueschel, S. M. (2000). *A Parent's Guide to Down Syndrome.* Baltimore: Paul H. Brookes.

Oppositional Behavior

Bronson, M. B. (2000). *Self-Regulation in Early Childhood: Nature and Nurture.* New York: Guilford.

Greene, R. W. (2001). *The Explosive Child: A New Approach for Understanding and Parenting Easily Frustrated and Chronically Inflexible Children.* New York: HarperCollins.

Greenspan, S. (1995). *The Challenging Child.* Reading, MA: Perseus Books.

Lynn, G. T. (2000). *Survival Strategies for Parenting Children with Bipolar Disorder.* London: Jessica Kingsley.

Physical Impairment

Gray, S. H., and Bloch, S. (2002). *Living with Cerebral Palsy.* Chanhassen, MN: Child's World.

Krementz, J. (1992). *How It Feels to Live with a Physical Disability.* New York: Simon & Schuster.

Lutkenhoff, M. (Ed.). (1999). *Children with Spina Bifida.* Bethesda, MD: Woodbine House.

Receptive Language Delay

Hamaguchi, P. A. (2001). *Childhood Speech, Language and Listening Problems.* New York: Wiley.

Newman, S. (1999). *Small Steps Forward: Using Games and Activities to Help Your Pre-School Child with Special Needs.* London: Jessica Kingsley.

School Entry Readiness

Anderson, S. S., and Honess, C. M. (1987). *Getting Ready for School: A Calendar of Practical Activities for School Readiness.* New York: Addison-Wesley.

Partakian, R. (2003). *Before the ABCs: Promoting School Readiness in Infants and Toddlers.* Washington, DC: Zero To Three.

Rawson, M., and Rose, M. (2002). *Ready to Learn: From Birth to School Readiness.* Portland, OR: Hawthorne Books.

Walmsley, B. B., and Walmsley, S. A. (1996). *Kindergarten: Ready or Not? A Parent's Guide.* Portsmouth, NH: Heinemann.

Wilkins, S. (2000). *Ready for Kindergarten.* Grand Rapids, MI: Zondervan.

Sensory Integration Needs

Biel, L., and Peske, N. (2005). *Raising a Sensory Smart Child: The Definitive Handbook for Helping Your Child with Sensory Integration Issues.* London: Penguin.
Chara, K. A., and Chara, P. J., Jr. (2004). *Sensory Smarts: A Book for Kids with ADHD or Autism Spectrum Disorders Struggling with Sensory Integration Problems.* London: Jessica Kingsley.
Kranowitz, C. S. (1998). *The Out-of-Sync Child.* New York: Skylight .
Kranowitz, C. S. (2003). *The Out-of-Sync Child Has Fun: Activities for Kids with Sensory Integration Dysfunction.* New York: Berkley Publishing Group.

Separation Anxiety

Dacey, J. S., and Fiore, L. B. (2000). *Your Anxious Child: How Parents and Teachers Can Relieve Anxiety in Children.* San Francisco: Jossey-Bass.
Manassis, K. (1996). *Keys to Parenting Your Anxious Child.* Hauppauge, NY: Barron's.
Minchella, N. (2003). *Mama Will Be Home Soon.* New York: Scholastic.

Shyness/Social Phobia

Manassis, K. (1996). *Keys to Parenting Your Anxious Child.* Hauppauge, NY: Barron's.
Swallow, W. K. (2000). *Shy Child: Helping Children Triumph over Shyness.* New York: Warner.

Sleep Issues

Ferber, R. (1985). *Solve Your Child's Sleep Problems.* New York: Simon & Schuster.
Mindell, J. A. (1997). *Sleeping through the Night: How Infants, Toddlers, and Their Parents Can Get a Good Night's Sleep.* New York: HarperCollins.
Weissbluth, M. (1999). *Healthy Sleep Habits, Happy Child.* New York: Ballantine.

Social Skills Delay

Mannix, D. (2002). *Social Skills Activities for Special Children.* Hoboken, NJ: Jossey-Bass.
Nelson, J., Erwin, C., and Duffy, R. (1998). *Positive Discipline for Preschoolers: For Their Early Years—Raising Children Who Are Responsible, Respectful and Resourceful.* Roseville, CA: Prima.

Shure, M. (1996). *Raising a Thinking Child: Help Your Child to Resolve Everyday Conflicts and Get Along With Others.* New York: Pocket Books.

Vision Deficits/Blindness

Harrison, F., and Crow, M. (1993). *Living and Learning with Blind Children: A Guide for Parents and Teachers of Visually Impaired Children.* Toronto: University of Toronto Press.
Holbrook, M. C. (Ed.). (1996). *Children with Visual Impairments: A Parent's Guide.* Bethesda, MD: Woodbine House.

Appendix B

PROFESSIONAL BIBLIOGRAPHY

Aggressive Behavior

Barkley, R. A. (1998). *Defiant Children, Second Edition: A Clinician's Manual for Assessment and Parent Training.* New York: Guilford.

Bloomquist, M. L., and Schnell, S. V. (2002). *Helping Children with Aggression and Conduct Problems: Best Practices for Intervention.* New York: Guilford.

Greene, R. W. (1998). *The Explosive Child.* New York: HarperCollins.

Lieberman, A. F., and Van Horn, P. (2004). Assessment and Treatment of Young Children Exposed to Traumatic Events. In J. D. Osofsky (Ed.), *Young Children and Trauma.* New York: Guilford.

Linder, T. W. (1990). *Transdisciplinary Play-Based Assessment: A Functional Approach to Working with Young Children.* Baltimore: Paul H. Brookes.

McGinnis, E., and Goldstein, A. P. (1990). *Skillstreaming in Early Childhood: Teaching Prosocial Skills to the Preschool and Kindergarten Child.* Champaign, IL: Research Press.

Mueller, F., and Larson, M. (2001). *Positive Behavior Support for Young Children: A Supplement to Positive Behavior for ALL Michigan Students: Creating Environments That Assure Learning.* Charlotte, MI: Center for Educational Networking, Eaton Intermediate School District.

Phelan, T. (1995). *1-2-3 Magic: Training Your Preschoolers and Preteens to Do What You Want.* Glen Ellyn, IL: Child Management.

Pinsonneault, I. L., Richardson, J. P., Jr., and Pinsonneault, J. (2002). Three Models of Educational Interventions for Child and Adolescent Firesetters. In D. Kolko (Ed.), *Handbook on Firesetting in Children and Youth.* San Diego, CA: Academic Press.

Stewart, J. (2002). *Beyond Time Out.* Gorham, ME: Hastings Clinical Associates.

Articulation/Voice Concerns

Camarata, S. M. (1995). A Rationale for Naturalistic Speech Intelligibility Intervention. In M. E. Fey, J. Windsor, and S. F. Warren (Eds.), *Language Intervention: Preschool through the Elementary Years* (pp. 63–84). Baltimore: Paul H. Brookes.

Crary, M. A. (1993). *Developmental Motor Speech Disorders.* San Diego, CA: Singular.

Dodd, B. (1995). *Differential Diagnosis and Treatment of Children with Speech Disorders.* San Diego, CA: Singular.

Marshalla, P. (2001). *Oral-Motor Techniques in Articulation and Phonological Therapy.* Kirkland, WA: Marshalla Speech and Language.

Peters, T. J., and Guitar, B. (1991). *Stuttering: An Integrated Approach to Its Nature and Treatment.* Baltimore: Williams and Wilkins.

Plante, E., and Beeson, P. M. (1999). *Communication and Communication Disorders.* Needham Heights, MA: Allyn & Bacon.

Rustin, L., Botterill, W., and Kelman, E. (1996). *Assessment and Therapy for Young Dysfluent Children.* San Diego, CA: Whurr.

Williams, A. L. (2003). *Speech Disorders Resource Guide for Preschool Children.* Clifton Park, NY: Thomson/Delmar Learning.

Attachment Concerns

Brisch, K. H. (2002). *Treating Attachment Disorders: From Theory to Therapy.* New York: Guilford.

Greenspan, S. L. (1992). *Infancy and Early Childhood: The Practice of Clinical Assessment and Intervention with Emotional and Developmental Challenges.* New York: International Universities Press.

Levy, T. M. (1998). *Attachment, Trauma, and Healing: Understanding and Treating Attachment Disorder in Children.* Washington, DC: CWLA Press.

Maldonado-Duran, J. M. (Ed.). (2002). *Infant and Toddler Mental Health.* Washington, DC: American Psychiatric.

Michigan Department of Education—Office of Special Education and Early Intervention Services. (2001). *Positive Behavior Support for Young Children.* Charlotte, MI: Eaton Intermediate School District.

Michigan Department of Education—Office of Special Education and Early Intervention Services. (2000). *Positive Behavior Support for ALL Michigan Students: Creating Environments That Assure Learning.* Charlotte, MI: Eaton Intermediate School District.

Solomon, J., and George, C. (1999). *Attachment Disorganization.* New York: Guilford.

Attention/Focus

De Gangi, G. (2000). *Pediatric Disorders of Regulation in Affect and Behavior.* San Diego, CA: Academic.

Gimpel, G. A., and Holland, M. L. (2003). *Emotional and Behavioral Problems of Young Children.* New York: Guilford.

Greenspan, S. L. (1992). *Infancy and Early Childhood: The Practice of Clinical Assessment and Intervention with Emotional and Developmental Challenges.* New York: International Universities Press.

Sandberg, S. (Ed.). (1996). *Hyperactivity Disorders of Childhood.* Cambridge, England: Cambridge University Press.

Schroeder, C. S., and Gordon, B. N. (2002). *Assessment and Treatment of Childhood Problems.* New York: Guilford.

Autism

Bondy, A., and Frost, L. (1985). *Picture Exchange Communication System (PECS).* Newark, DE: Pyramid Educational Consultants.

Cohen, S. (1998). *Targeting Autism: What We Know, Don't Know, and Can Do to Help Young Children with Autism and Related Disorders.* Los Angeles: University of California Press.

Greenspan, S. I., and Wieder, S. (1997). An Integrated Developmental Approach to Interventions for Young Children with Severe Difficulties in Relating and Communicating. *Zero To Three, 17,* 5–18.

Handleman, J. S., and Harris, S. L. (Eds.). (2001). *Preschool Education Programs for Children with Autism.* Austin, TX: Pro-Ed.

McClannahan, L. E., and Krantz, P. J. (1999). *Activity Schedules for Children with Autism: Teaching Independent Behavior.* Bethesda, MD: Woodbine House.

Mesibov, G., Shea, V., and Schopler, E. (2004). *The TEACCH Approach to Autism Spectrum Disorders.* New York: Plenum.

Mueller, F., and Larson, M. (2001). *Positive Behavior Support for Young Children: A Supplement to Positive Behavior for ALL Michigan Students: Creating Environments That Assure Learning.* Charlotte, MI: Center for Educational Networking, Eaton Intermediate School District.

Ozonoff, S., Rogers, S. J., and Hendren, R. (Eds.). (2003). *Autism Spectrum Disorders: A Research Review for Practitioners.* New York: American Psychiatric Association.

Powell, S. (2000). *Helping Children with Autism to Learn.* London: David Fulton.

Prizant, B. M., Wetheroy, A. M., Rubin, E., Laurent, A. C., and Rydell, P. J. (2005). *The SCERTS Model: A Comprehensive Educational Approach for Children with Autism Spectrum Disorders.* Baltimore: Brookes.

Scheuermann, B., and Webber, J. (2002). *Autism: Teaching Does Make a Difference.* Belmont, CA: Wadsworth/Thomson Learning.

Weiss, M. J., and Harris, S. L. (2001). *Reaching Out, Joining IN: Teaching Social Skills to Young Children with Autism.* Bethesda, MD: Woodbine House.

Wolfberg, P. J. (1999). *Play and Imagination in Children with Autism.* New York: Teachers College Press.

Depression

Dubuque, S. E. (1996). *Survival Guide to Childhood Depression.* Plainview, NY: Childswork/Childsplay.
Elliott, J., and Place, M. (1998). *Children in Difficulty: A Guide to Understanding and Helping.* New York: Routledge.
Fassler, D. G., and Dumas, L. S. (1998). *"Help Me, I'm Sad": Recognizing, Treating, and Preventing Childhood and Adolescent Depression.* New York: Penguin.
Gimpel, G. A., and Holland, M. L. (2003). *Emotional and Behavioral Problems of Young Children.* New York: Guilford.
Greenspan, S. L. (1992). *Infancy and Early Childhood: The Practice of Clinical Assessment and Intervention with Emotional and Developmental Challenges.* New York: International Universities Press.
Trad, P. V. (1987). *Infant and Childhood Depression.* New York: Wiley.

Eating Concerns

Gimpel, G. A., and Holland, M. L. (2003). *Emotional and Behavioral Problems of Young Children.* New York: Guilford.
Kedesdy, J. H., and Budd, K. S. (1998). *Childhood Feeding Disorders: Bio-behavioral Assessment and Intervention.* Baltimore: Brookes.
Kessler, D. B., and Dawson, P. (1999). *Failure to Thrive and Pediatric Under-nutrition.* Baltimore: Brookes.
Schroeder, C. S., and Gordon, B. N. (2002). *Assessment and Treatment of Childhood Problems.* New York: Guilford.

Elimination Concerns

Buchanan, A., in collaboration with G. Clayden (1992). *Children Who Soil: Assessment and Treatment.* New York: Wiley.
Gimpel, G. A., and Holland, M. L. (2003). *Emotional and Behavioral Problems of Young Children.* New York: Guilford.
Klykylo, W. M., Kay, J. and Rube, J. (1998). *Clinical Child Psychiatry.* Philadelphia: W. B. Saunders.
Schaefer, C. E. (1993). *Childhood Encopresis and Enuresis: Causes and Therapy.* Lanham, MD: Rowman & Littlefield.
Schroeder, C. S., and Gordon, B. N. (2002). *Assessment and Treatment of Childhood Problems.* New York: Guilford.

Expressive Language Delay

Cantwell, D., and Baker, L. (1987). *Developmental Speech and Language Disorders.* New York: Guilford.

Fey, M. E., Windsor, J., and Warren, S. F. (1995). *Language Intervention— Preschool through the Elementary Years.* Baltimore: Paul H. Brookes.

Griffiths, F. (2002). *Communication Counts: Speech and Language Difficulties in the Early Years.* London: David Fulton.

Justice, L. M. (2004). Creating Language-Rich Preschool Classroom Environments. *Teaching Exceptional Children, 37,* 36–44.

Weiss, A. L. (2001). *Preschool Language Disorders Resource Guide.* San Diego, CA: Singular/Thomson Learning.

Generalized Anxiety

Carducci, B. J. (1999). *Shyness: A Bold New Approach.* New York: HarperCollins.

Dragonwagon, C. (2003). *Bat in the Dining Room.* Salt Lake City, UT: Benchmark.

Ellis, A. (1961). *New Guide to Rational Living.* New York: Wehman Brothers.

Emberley, E. (1993). *Go Away Big Green Monster.* New York: Little, Brown.

Falcover, I. (2003). *Olivia and the Missing Toy.* New York: Atheneum.

Gardner, R. A. (1993). *Storytelling in Psychotherapy with Children.* Lanham, MD: Jason Aronson.

Henkes, K. (2000). *Wemberly Worried.* New York: Greenwillow.

Howard, A. (1999). *When I Was Five.* New York: Harcourt.

Huberty, T. J. (1997). Anxiety. In G. G. Bear, K. M. Minke, and A. Thomas (Eds.), *Children's Needs II: Development, Problems and Alternatives.* Bethesda, MD: NASP Publications.

Hughes, S. (1981). *Alfie Gets in First.* Englewood, CO: Mulberry Hill.

Hughes, S. (1997). *All about Alfie.* New York: Lothrop Lee & Shepard.

Ollendick, T. H., and Cerny, J. A. (1981). *Clinical Behavior Therapy with Children.* New York: Plenum.

Waddell, M. (1992). *Owl Babies.* Cambridge, MA: Candlewick.

Hearing Deficits/Deafness

Bodner-Johnson, B., and Sass-Lehrer, M. (Eds.). (2003). *The Young Deaf or Hard of Hearing Child: A Family Centered Approach to Early Education.* Baltimore: Paul H. Brookes.

Butler, K. G. (1994). *Hearing Impairment and Language Disorders: Assessment and Intervention.* Gaithersburg, MD: Aspen.

Flexer, C. (1999). *Facilitating Hearing and Listening in Young Children.* San Diego, CA: Singular.

Luetke-Stahlman, B., and Luchner, J. (1990). *Effectively Educating Students with Hearing Impairments.* White Plains, NY: Longman.

Marschark, M. (1993). *Psychological Development of Deaf Children.* New York: Oxford University Press.

Maxon, A. B., and Brackett, D. (1992). *The Hearing-Impaired Child: Infancy through High School Years.* Boston: Andover Medical.

National Information Center on Deafness. (1991). *Mainstreaming Deaf and Hard of Hearing Students.* Washington, DC: Gallaudet University Press.

Northern, J. L., and Downs, M. P. (2002). *Hearing in Children.* Baltimore: Lippincott Williams & Wilkins.

Pappas, D. G. (1998). *Diagnosis and Treatment of Hearing Impairment in Children.* San Diego, CA: Singular.

Plante, E., and Beeson, P. M. (1999). *Communication and Communication Disorders.* Needham Heights, MA: Allyn & Bacon.

Ripley, K., Barrett, J., and Fleming, P. (2001). *Inclusion for Children with Speech and Language Impairments.* London: David Fulton.

Sindrey, D. (1997). *Listening Games for Littles.* London, Canada: Word Play.

Medically Fragile

Hayman, L. L., Mahon, M. M., and Turner, J. R. (2002). *Chronic Illness in Children.* New York: Springer.

Jackson, P. L., and Versey, A. (2000). *Primary Care of the Child with a Chronic Condition.* St. Louis, MO: Mosby.

Mesec, A. L., and Fraser, C. H. (1997). *Serious Illness in the Classroom.* Englewood, CO: Teacher Ideas.

Wishnietsky, D. B., and Wishnietsky, D. H. (1996). *Managing Chronic Pain in the Classroom.* Bloomington, IN: Phi Delta Kappa Educational Foundation.

Mild Cognitive Delays

Allen, K. E. (1992). *The Exceptional Child: Mainstreaming in Early Childhood Education.* Albany, NY: Delmar.

Beckman, P. J., Hanson, M. J., Horn, E., Lieber, J., Sandall, S. R., Schwartz, I. S., and Wolery, R. A. (2002). In S. L. Odom (Ed.), *Widening the Circle: Including Children with Disabilities in Preschool Programs.* New York: Teachers College.

Hodapp, R. M. (1998). *Development and Disabilities: Intellectual, Sensory and Motor Impairments.* Cambridge, England: Cambridge University Press.

Odom, Zercher, Marquart, Li, Sandall, and Wolfberg. (2002). Social Relationships of Children with Disabilities and Their Peers in Inclusive Preschool Classrooms. In S. L. Odom (Ed.), *Widening the Circle: Including Children with Disabilities in Preschool Programs.* New York: Teachers College.

Porter, L. (2002). *Educating Young Children with Special Needs.* Crows Nest, Australia: Paul Chapman.

Stull-Barnes, K. (1987). *Mainstreaming Young Children with Mild Mental Retardation in the Regular Preschool Setting.* Toledo, OH: University of Toledo.

Tingey, C. (Ed.). (1988). *Down Syndrome: A Resource Handbook.* Boston, MA: College-Hill Publication.

Wilson, R. A. (1998). *Special Educational Needs in the Early Years.* New York: Routledge.

Moderate/Severe Cognitive Impairment

Gargiulo, R., and Kilgo, J. L. (2004). *Young Children with Special Needs.* Albany, NY: Delmar.

Horn, E., Lieber, J., Sandall, S. R., Schwartz, I. S., and Wolery, R. A. (2002). Classroom Models of Individualized Instruction. In S. L. Odom (Ed.), *Widening the Circle: Including Children with Disabilities in Preschool Programs.* New York: Teachers College.

Johnson-Martin, N. M., Jens, K. G., Attermeier, S. M., and Hacker, B. J. (1990). *The Carolina Curriculum for Preschoolers with Special Needs.* Baltimore: Paul H. Brookes.

McCormick, L., and Feeney, S. (1995). Modifying and Expanding Activities for Children with Disabilities. *Young Children, 50,* 10–17.

Odom, S. L. (2002). Classroom Models of Individualized Instruction. In E. Horn (Ed.), *Widening the Circle: Including Children with Disabilities in Preschool Programs.* New York: Teachers College.

Porter, L. (2002). *Educating Young Children with Special Needs.* Crows Nest, Australia: Paul Chapman.

Sandall, S., Schwartz, I., Joseph, G., Chou, H. Y., Horn, E., Lieber, J., Odom, S., and Wolery, R. A. (2002). *Building Blocks for Successful Early Childhood Programs: Strategies for Including All Children.* Baltimore, MD: Paul H. Brookes.

Westling, D. L., and Fox, L. (1995). *Teaching Students with Severe Disabilities.* Englewood Cliffs, NJ: Merrill.

Oppositional Behavior

Barkley, R. A. (1998). *Defiant Children, Second Edition: A Clinician's Manual for Assessment and Parent Training.* New York: Guilford.

Brenner, M. L. (1998). *When "No" Gets You Nowhere: Teaching Your Toddler and Child Self-Control.* Rocklin, CA: Prima.

Gimpel, G. A., and Holland, M. L. (2003). *Emotional and Behavioral Problems of Young Children.* New York: Guilford.

Greene, R. W. (1998). *The Explosive Child.* New York: HarperCollins.

McGinnis, E., and Goldstein, A. P. (1990). *Skillstreaming in Early Childhood: Teaching Prosocial Skills to the Preschool and Kindergarten Child.* Champaign, IL: Research Press.

McMahon, R. J., and Forehand, R. L. (2003). *Helping the Noncompliant Child.* New York: Guilford.

Michigan Department of Education—Office of Special Education and Early Intervention Services. (2001). *Positive Behavior Support for Young Children.* Charlotte, MI: Eaton Intermediate School District.

Michigan Department of Education—Office of Special Education and Early Intervention Services. (2000). *Positive Behavior Support for ALL Michigan Students: Creating Environments That Assure Learning.* Charlotte, MI: Eaton Intermediate School District.

Phelan, T. (1995). *1-2-3 Magic: Training Your Preschoolers and Preteens to Do What You Want.* Glen Ellyn, IL: Child Management.

Stewart, J. (2002). *Beyond Time Out.* Gorham, ME: Hastings Clinical Associates.

Physical Impairment

Bigge, J. L. (1991). *Teaching Individuals with Physical and Multiple Disabilities.* New York: Merrill/Macmillan.

Bondy, A., and Frost, L. (1985). *Picture Exchange Communication System (PECS).* Newark, DE: Pyramid Educational Consultants.

Gould, P., and Sullivan, J. (1999). *The Inclusive Early Childhood Classroom: Easy Ways to Adapt Learning Centers for All Children.* Beltsville, MD: Gryphon House.

Klein, M. D., Cook, R. E., and Richardson-Gibbs, A. M. (2000). *Strategies for Including Children with Special Needs in Early Childhood Settings.* Albany, NY: Delmar.

Paasche, C. L., Gorrill, L., and Strom, B. (2004). *Children with Special Needs in Early Childhood Settings.* Clifton Park, NY: Delmar.

Ross, A. O. (1964). *The Exceptional Child in the Family.* New York: Grune & Stratton.

Wilson, R. A. (1998). *Special Educational Needs in the Early Years.* New York: Routledge.

Winkelstern, J. A., and Jongsma, A. E., Jr. (2001). *The Special Education Treatment Planner.* New York: Wiley.

School Entry Readiness

Boyer, E. L. (1991). *Ready To Learn: A Mandate for the Nation.* Princeton, NJ: Carnegie Foundation for the Advancement of Teaching.

Fabian, H., and Dunlop, A. W. (Eds.). (2002). *Transitions in the Early Years.* New York: Routledge Falmer.

Gestwicki, C. (2004). *Home, School, and Community Relations: A Guide to Working with Families.* Clifton Park, NY: Delmar.

Graue, M. E. (1993). *Ready for What? Constructing Meanings of Readiness for Kindergarten.* Albany, NY: State University of New York Press.

Hazen, N., Black, B., and Fleming-Johnson, F. (1984). Social Acceptance: Strategies Children Use and How Teachers Can Help Children Learn Them. *Young Children, 39,* 23–26.

McLanaham, S., and Haskins, R. (2005). *School Readiness: Closing the Racial and Ethnic Gaps.* Washington, DC: Brookings Institution.

Sandall, S. R., and Schwartz, I. S. (2002). *Building Blocks for Teaching Preschoolers with Special Needs.* Baltimore: Paul H. Brookes.

Sornson, B. (Ed.) (2001). *Preventing Early Learning Failure.* Alexandria, VA: Association for Supervision and Curriculum Development.

Steele, W., and Couillard, J. (1995). *Violence Prevention and Intervention Readiness for Schools.* Indianapolis, IN: Kidsrights.

Sensory Integration Needs

Ayres, A. J. (1980). *Sensory Integration and the Child.* Los Angeles: Western Psychological Services.

De Gangi, G. (2000). *Pediatric Disorders of Regulation in Affect and Behavior.* San Diego, CA: Academic.

Heller, S. (2003). *Too Loud, Too Bright, Too Fast, Too Tight: What To Do If You Are Sensory Defensive In an Overstimulating World.* New York: HarperCollins.

Kranowitz, C. S., Sava, D. I., Haber, E., Balzer-Martin, L., and Szhlut, S. (2001). *Answers to Questions Teachers Ask about Sensory Integration.* Las Vegas, NV: Sensory Resources.

Matson, J., Fee, V., Coe, D., and Smith, D. (1991). A Social Skills Program for Developmentally Delayed Preschoolers. *Child and Family Behavior Therapy, 20,* 227–242.

Smith, K. A., and Gouge, K. R. (2004). *The Sensory-Sensitive Child: Practical Solutions for Out-of-Bounds Behavior.* New York: HarperCollins.

Yack, E., Sutton, S., and Aquilla, P. (2003). *Building Bridges through Sensory Integration—Second Edition.* Las Vegas, NV: Sensory Resources.

Separation Anxiety

Achenbach, T. (2003). *Achenbach System of Empirically Based Assessment (Preschool Age).* San Antonio, TX: Harcourt Assessment.

Carducci, B. J. (2003). *The Shyness Breakthrough.* New York: Rodale.

Klein, M. D., Cook, R. E., and Richardson-Gibbs, A. M. (2000). *Strategies for Including Children with Special Needs in Early Childhood Settings.* Albany, NY: Delmar.

Ollendick, T. H., and Cerny, J. A. (1981). *Clinical Behavior Therapy with Children.* New York: Plenum.

Schneider, M., and Robin, A. (1976). The Turtle Technique: A Method for the

Self-Control of Impulsive Behavior. In J. Krumboltz and C. Thoreson (Eds.), *Counseling Methods* (pp. 157–162). New York: Hold, Rinehart, & Winston.

Shyness/Social Phobia

Carducci, B. J. (1999). *Shyness: A Bold New Approach*. New York: HarperCollins.
Carducci, B. J. (2003). *The Shyness Breakthrough*. New York: Rodale.
Crozier, W. R. (2000). *Shyness: Development, Consolidation and Change*. New York: Routledge.
Crozier, W. R. (2001). *Understanding Shyness: Psychological Perspectives*. New York: Palgrave.
Ollendick, T. H., and Cerny, J. A. (1981). *Clinical Behavior Therapy with Children*. New York: Plenum.
Zimbardo, P. G., and Radl, S. L. (1999).*The Shy Child: Overcoming and Preventing Shyness from Infancy to Adulthood*. New York: McGraw Hill.

Sleep Issues

Firman, P. C., Hoff, K. E., Schnoes, C., Freeman, K. A., Woods, D. W., and Blum, N. (1999). The Bedtime Pass: An Approach to Bedtime Crying and Leaving the Room. *Archives of Pediatric and Adolescent Medicine, 153,* 1027–1029.
Gimpel, G. A., and Holland, M. L. (2003). *Emotional and Behavioral Problems of Young Children*. New York: Guilford.
Maldonado-Duran, J. M. (Ed.). (2002). *Infant and Toddler Mental Health*. Washington, DC: American Psychiatric.
Stores, G., and Wiggs, L. (2001). *Sleep Disturbance in Children and Adolescents with Disorders of Development: Its Significance and Management*. London: Mac Keith.

Social Skills Delay

Barkley, R. A. (1997). *Defiant Children, Second Edition: A Clinician's Manual for Assessment and Parent Training*. New York: Guilford.
Charney, R. S., and Wood, C. (1981). *The Responsible Classroom Approach to Instruction*. Greenfield, MA: Northeast Foundation for Children.
Delton, J. (1988). *Two Good Friends*. New York: Knopf Books for Young Readers.
Elliott, S. N., McKevitt, B. C., and DePerna, J. C. (2002). Preschool Social Skills Training. In A. Thomas and J. Grimes (Eds.), *Best Practices in School Psychology IV* (pp. 1041–1056). Bethesda, Maryland: National Association of School Psychologists.
Fay, J., and Fay, C. (2002). *Love and Logic Magic for Early Childhood: Practical Parentng from Birth to Six Years*. Golden, CO: Love and Logic.

Gresham, F. M., and Elliott, S. N. (1990). *The Social Skills Rating System.* Circle Pines, MN: American Guidance Services.

Hazen, N., Black, B., and Fleming-Johnson, F. (1984). Social Acceptance: Strategies Children Use and How Teachers Can Help Children Learn Them. *Young Children, 39,* 23–26.

LaRoque, M., Brown, S., and Johnson, K. (2001). Functional Behavioral Assessments and Intervention Plans in Early Intervention Settings. *Infants and Young Children, 13,* 59–68.

Matson, J., Fee, V., Coe, D., and Smith, D. (1991). A Social Skills Program for Developmentally Delayed Preschoolers. *Child and Family Behavior Therapy, 20,* 227–242.

Merrell, K. W. (1994). *Preschool and Kindergarten Behavior Scales.* Austin, TX: Pro-Ed.

Michigan Department of Education—Office of Special Education and Early Intervention Services. (2000). *Positive Behavior Support for ALL Michigan Students: Creating Environments That Assure Learning.* Charlotte, MI: Eaton Intermediate School District.

Mueller, F., and Larson, M. (2001). *Positive Behavior Support for Young Children: A Supplement to Positive Behavior Support for ALL Michigan Students: Creating Environments That Assure Learning.* Charlotte, MI: Eaton Intermediate School District.

Phelan, T. (1995). *1-2-3 Magic: Training Your Preschoolers and Preteens to Do What You Want.* Glen Ellyn, IL: Child Management.

Prutzman, P., Burger, M. L., Bodenhamer, G., and Stern, L. (1977). *The Friendly Classroom for a Small Planet: Handbook of the Children's Creative Response to Conflict Program.* New York: Quaker Project on Community Conflict.

Vision Deficits/Blindness

Pogrund, R. L., Fazzi, D. L., and Lampert, J. S. (1992). *Early Focus: Working with Young Blind and Visually Impaired Children and Their Families.* New York: American Foundation for the Blind.

Sachs, S. Z., Kekelis, L. S., and Gaylord-Ross, R. J. (1992). *The Development of Social Skills by Blind and Visually Impaired Students.* New York: American Foundation for the Blind.

Stratton, J. M., and Wright, S. (1991). *On the Way to Literacy: Early Experiences for Visually Impaired Children.* Louisville, KY: American Printing House for the Blind.

Trief, E. (1992). *Working with Visually Impaired Young Students: A Curriculum Guide for Birth–3 Year Olds.* Springfield, IL: Charles C. Thomas.

Webster, A., and Roe, J. (1998). *Children with Visual Impairments: Social Interaction, Language and Learning.* New York: Routledge.